For the Good of
the Earth and Sun

For
the Good of
the Earth and
Sun

Teaching Poetry

Georgia Heard

With a Foreword by
LUCY McCORMICK CALKINS

HEINEMANN
Portsmouth, New Hampshire

Heinemann

A division of Reed Elsevier Inc.

361 Hanover Street, Portsmouth, NH 03801-3912

Offices and agents throughout the world

The publisher and author wish to thank the children and their parents for permission to reproduce the children's work, and the following for permission to quote from previously published works:

Page 3: Excerpt from "Open House" copyright 1941 by Theodore Roethke, from *The Collected Poems of Theodore Roethke*. Reprinted by permission of Doubleday, a division of Bantam, Doubleday, Dell Publishing Group, Inc.

Page 8: Reprinted from *Next to Last Things* by Stanley Kunitz. Copyright © 1985 by Stanley Kunitz. By permission of the Atlantic Monthly Press.

Page 26: "April Rain Song." Copyright 1932 by Alfred A. Knopf, Inc. and renewed 1960 by Langston Hughes. Reprinted from *The Dream Keeper and Other Poems* by Langston Hughes, by permission of the publisher.

Page 27: "Things" from *Honey, I Love and Other Love Poems* by Eloise Greenfield. (Thomas Y. Crowell) Text copyright © 1978 by Eloise Greenfield. Reprinted by permission of Harper & Row, Publishers, Inc.

Page 44: Reprinted from "Writing off the Subject" from *The Triggering Town, Lectures and Essays on Poetry and Writing* by Richard Hugo, by permission of W. W. Norton & Company, Inc. Copyright © 1979 by W. W. Norton & Company, Inc.

Pages 55–56: "We Real Cool." From *The World of Gwendolyn Brooks*. Copyright © 1959 by Gwendolyn Brooks Blakely. Reprinted by permission of the author.

Page 59: "Poem" from William Carlos Williams, *Collected Poems 1909–1939, Vol. 1*. Copyright 1938 by New Directions Publishing Corporation. Reprinted by permission of New Directions Publishing Corporation.

Page 66: "Apple" by Nan Fry. Reprinted by permission of *Plainsong*.

Page 67: "The Dark Gray Clouds" from *The Sun Is a Golden Earring* by Natalia M. Belting. Copyright © 1962 by Natalia M. Belting. Reprinted by permission of Henry Holt and Company, Inc.

Page 70: Excerpt from "Mr. Edwards and the Spider" from *Lord Weary's Castle*, copyright 1946 and renewed 1974 by Robert Lowell, reprinted by permission of Harcourt Brace Jovanovich, Inc.

Page 85: "To a Poor Old Woman" from William Carlos Williams, *Collected Poems 1909–1939, Vol. 1*. Copyright 1938 by New Directions Publishing Corporation. Reprinted by permission of New Directions Publishing Corporation.

Pages 90–91: "Sestina" from *The Complete Poems* by Elizabeth Bishop. Copyright © 1983 by Alice Helen Methfessal. Copyright © 1956 by Elizabeth Bishop. Reprinted by permission of Farrar, Straus & Giroux, Inc.

Page 95: "Villanelle" by Jean Passerat (English translation by Mary Logue) is reprinted from *The Teachers & Writers Handbook of Poetic Forms*, copyright © 1987 by Teachers & Writers Collaborative. Used by permission of Teachers & Writers Collaborative.

Pages 133–34, 135–36: "Mother to Son" and "I, Too." Copyright 1926 by Alfred A. Knopf, Inc. and renewed 1954 by Langston Hughes. Reprinted from *Selected Poems of Langston Hughes*, by permission of the publisher.

Every effort has been made to contact the copyright holders and the children and their parents for permission to reprint borrowed material. We regret any oversights that may have occurred and would be happy to rectify them in future printings of this work.

Library of Congress Cataloging-in-Publication Data

Heard, Georgia.

    For the good of the earth and sun : teaching poetry / Georgia Heard ; with a foreword by Lucy McCormick Calkins.

      p.   cm.

    Includes bibliographies.

    ISBN 0-435-08495-X

    1. Poetry—Study and teaching (Elementary)   I. Title.

PN1101.H4   1989   88-35969

372.6'4—dc19   CIP

Front-cover illustration from a drawing by Jonathan Floril. Back-cover photo by Dianne Repp. Designed by Wladislaw Finne.

Printed in the United States of America.

10 9

For the kids of the New York City schools

Have you reckoned a thousand acres much? Have you reckoned the earth much?
Have you practiced so long to learn to read?
Have you felt so proud to get at the meaning of poems?

Stop this day and night with me and you shall possess the origin of all poems,
You shall possess the good of the earth and sun—there are millions of suns left,
You shall no longer take things at second or third hand, nor look through the eyes of
the dead, nor feed on the spectres in books,
You shall not look through my eyes either, nor take things from me,
You shall listen to all sides and filter them from yourself.

Walt Whitman
from "Song of Myself"

Contents

Five
Language: The Poet's Paint   65

Six
Tennis and Racquetball: On Form   75

Seven
"The Sun Is Like a Mommy": Kindergarten and First Grade   99

Eight
Making a World of Poetry: Rituals   125

Appendix
Anthology of Poems by Children   139

Bibliographies

Foreword

Lucy McCormick Calkins

Reading *For the Good of the Earth and Sun,* one is struck first by the
realization that this is not a book on teaching poetry but on teaching reading
and writing, and even on teaching itself. As I read it, my first and most
overwhelming response was "God, this is big." It's big the way Eudora
Welty's *One Writer's Beginnings* is big, the way Anne Morrow Lindbergh's
A Gift from the Sea is big.

Georgia looks closely at the littlest details of reading and writing classrooms and finds in them important truths. She talks about choosing poems
to read aloud and says, "I look for poems as varied as trees or flowers or
the many different faces on city streets—poems that tell the truth about the
world." She talks about the arrangements of a writing classroom and says,
"There are places that give me an excited urge to write, places that feel rich
and warm, where time slows down and whatever I want to do is possible. . . . Sometimes when I was a girl my mother would cook a turkey on
Sunday; the smells permeated the house as I lay upstairs on my bed reading
and gave me [a] feeling of peace. It's important that classrooms have this
richness."

Georgia's wisdom is conveyed not only by what she says, but also by the
way she writes. There is no one in the field who writes like this. We talk
about taking time to listen, to look, but as I think about the great books on
teaching writing, I do not know of any other author who takes the time to

describe a boy's miniature face, a girl's deep, dark eyes, a five-year-old who reads her poem standing up very tall, her chin in the air, slowly saying her poem, measuring her words.

Because I know that this book has come from hundreds of children, spread over six years of work, I recently asked Georgia whether she creates these details in order to buoy up her writing, deciding as she writes that Reginald might have had a plump face and Erin, large hands. "Oh, no," she said. "I remember their faces, their hands." And that, I realized, is the reason these descriptions matter. They keep Georgia's attention on the true moments in classrooms and, in this way, they keep her writing honest and accountable to real life.

Readers of *The Art of Teaching Writing* will remember Georgia Heard. Georgia's chapter on poetry stands out from all the others in that book because instead of threading ideas about teaching writing through a patchwork of classrooms, I simply move out of the way and let readers witness the magic of Georgia's work with a single class. The chapter opens with Georgia calling a class of New York City children together. "For me," she says once the youngsters have settled on the floor around her, "poems have to be about something that is so important to me, I need to have a physical feeling of that topic inside me." As the chapter unfolds, the children are drawn in, spellbound, by Georgia's struggles to dig inside her life and her writing in order to tell the truth about poetry. We readers are drawn in with the children.

For many of us, Georgia's wise work with those children has guided our teaching for a long time now. But for Georgia, the teaching described in that chapter represents only the beginning of her study of children and poetry.

Since that day six years ago, when Georgia gathered together the children from P.S. 230 to tell them about poetry, she has worked in hundreds of classrooms, with first graders and graduate students, with picture books and paintings, at science centers and author celebrations. As a member of the Teachers College Writing Project staff, she was for several years part of a team of educators that has been pushing the frontiers of knowledge on teaching reading as well as writing, on author studies, conferring, writers' notebooks, share sessions, and the like. Through all of this, Georgia has continued digging into the well of her own living and writing in order to tell the truth about poetry. Now all those years, all those experiences, all those teachers and children and poems have come together in this book.

For the Good of the Earth and Sun resonates with an uncommon depth. The book is deep and alive and important because it comes not from

deskwork and dusty theories, but from childhood worlds, love affairs, lifetime fears, long summers in a New Hampshire cabin, and Saturday morn-
ings in sunny New York bookstores. It has grown, layer by layer, out of all
her life.

Georgia's methods of teaching, like her book, have grown out of all her
life. She helps children collect anthologies of treasured poems because she
has poetry scrapbooks of her own. She encourages teachers and children to
hang poetry near the science corner, the coatrack, the unifix cubes, because
she has poems pasted on her bathroom mirror and poems tucked inside the
covers of the novels she reads. She helps children write poems that are
deeply true because she writes poems that resonate from her own experience. Georgia's teaching is inseparable from her living, and that is what
gives the book its scope and significance.

Acknowledgments

Every night when I was a little girl, before I went to bed, I'd kneel and say my prayers, thanking everyone I knew and loved in the world. That one prayer of gratitude would take so long my knees would start to ache; I had to make sure not to leave anyone out, so no one's feelings would be hurt. It wasn't until I'd named everyone that my conscience was clear and I'd finally sign off, climb into bed, and go to sleep.

Writing these acknowledgments feels a little like that. There have been so many people in my life who've helped, encouraged, and supported me; I could go on for pages. What follows is a partial list. I'm also grateful to many whose names don't appear on it.

My first thanks go to Lucy Calkins. When I first discovered her, I was a poetry student at Columbia University. One night after class she invited me to a café to talk about poetry; I didn't know it at the time, but it was there that this book was born. Shortly afterwards Lucy invited me to join the Teachers College Writing Project as a teacher of writing. I am grateful to Lucy for having created opportunities for me to grow as a teacher and for her knowledge, faith, and friendship over the past six years.

I'd also like to thank Shelley Harwayne, the assistant director of the Writing Project, whom I watched working brilliantly with students and teachers during the half year I shadowed her as a researcher. From her I learned how to teach and work with children; she's also been an invaluable source of wonderful quotes, new books and articles, and encouragement.

Every Thursday for the past four years, my colleagues at the Teachers College Writing Project and I have met and talked about ideas, then gone out to lunch and talked some more about our frustrations and hopes. I've made lifelong friends there; this book is filled with ideas that originated in those talks. JoAnn Curtis, Ralph Fletcher, Jenifer Hall, Martha Horn, Karen Howell, Hindy List, and Jim Sullivan were some of the original members of the Writing Project; I can't imagine any of this work without them. More recently, Dorothy Barnhouse, Elizabeth Henley, Drew Lamb, Andrea Lowenkopf, and Susan Stires have each informed, surprised, and inspired me more than I can say, and I thank them.

It would be impossible to list the names of all the New York City teachers and principals who have helped with the writing of this book. They are the most loyal and hardworking people I have ever known. Without the courage these dedicated people have given me and their questions and jokes, the growth of the ideas here would not have been possible. Many thanks also go to Beverly Barton, for her research, and to the teachers at the Putnam Valley Elementary School in upstate New York, the Amherst, Massachusetts public schools, and the Campton School in New Hampshire.

I'm also grateful to the community of poets. My teacher, Stanley Kunitz, saw in me what I couldn't yet see in myself when I was a student at Columbia. Annual visits to his house to talk about my poems have helped give me the courage to continue writing. I'm also grateful to Marie Howe and Candice Reffe, two fellow poets, for their faith and friendship at Columbia and now.

More recently, Don Graves, whose ideas I've been discovering for a long time, has given me good advice, poems, and great letters and phone conversations, and Philippa Stratton and Toby Gordon, my editors, have waited patiently and encouragingly for my first sketchy chapters to become this book.

Finally, I'd like to thank my friend the poet Suzanne Gardinier, who visited me last summer in Vermont, read the drafts of the first two chapters, and loved them. When I read them now I realize what an act of love that was and how much I needed it in order to find the time and the courage to write this. Over the year she has read everything, laughed at all the right places, and been a painstaking editor. I will never be able to thank her enough.

Thanks to all these extraordinary people, and to so many more I can't name.

Introduction

DIGGING THROUGH THE LAYERS

When I was a child, my family would escape the stifling heat of the Virginia summer for two weeks of cool air at my grandparents' house in a small New Hampshire town. I looked forward to these visits every year. It was there that poetry first touched me.

From the porch we could see Mount Chocorua; I would watch how its colors changed, from early morning blue to soft violet at sunset. Around the house were fields of grass and hay and large rocks we could stand on to become the highest humans for miles around. The property was threaded with old stone walls and surrounded by acres and acres of woods littered with mounds of stones whose origin, to me, was a mystery.

One day I asked my grandfather if he would walk with me in the woods. When we came across a mound of stones, I asked if he knew what it was. He told me that a long time ago, when the Indians lived on this land, they had used piles of stones to mark the graves of their dead.

My grandfather was prone to teasing and by this time I had already become a skeptic, so I suspected this might be one of his stories. But for days afterward I thought about those Indian graves. One day I decided to find out for myself whether or not he was telling the truth. I took a shovel from the tool shed and went into the woods to dig.

When I said that poetry first touched me at my grandparents' house, I meant that I felt there for the first time an unyielding curiosity, a solitary need to look for the truth. This has become a metaphor for writing poetry that has stayed with me all my life. In the woods, I cleared the stones away and dug in the dirt, sifting through the sacred grave to find whatever it had to tell me. As I think about those Indian graves now, I feel in them a sacredness that I would never dream of violating, partly because of my growth as a poet and a person. In the poems I've written since, my materials have changed, but the process is the same as I used that afternoon.

Not surprisingly, one of the first poems I ever wrote is about the Indian grave. It was years after my grandfather had died. The memory came rushing back to me, and I felt compelled to write it down.

Oldfields

1

I went out to see the Indian grave
my grandfather told me about
at the edge of the woods
near the burning field.

I picked off the leaves and stones
that covered the mound
and dug all afternoon
until the woods grew dark
and the kitchen light of the house
behind me came on.

I expected to find jewels,
pots and arrows
or an Indian headdress
with feathers in it.

Except for the dirt
that filtered through my hands,
the grave was empty.

2

I am standing near the wall
at the edge of the burning field.
I see my grandfather
walk around the rooms
of the empty summer house.
He has been dead for years.

Hunched over, thin as air,
he walks a path from the kitchen
through the dining room.

3

Years ago,
up the front staircase
in my bedroom in the summer house
I lay in bed awake
listening for the clock
downstairs to strike midnight.
I saw the spirits fly out of the clock
like black smoke going up a fan.

4

In the living room
the grandfather clock
is still ticking.

Any hour now,
it will break into chime.

When I was in college I took a poetry workshop with Robert Bly; one
night we met at a woman's house in Bethesda, Maryland, to write. We sat
around a dining room table where Bly scattered about a dozen onions. We
were each to peel an onion, looking carefully at each layer, writing in our
journals about what we noticed, like scientists. But we were also to think
about our childhoods, our mothers, our fathers, our lives as we slowly
peeled away each layer. It was an exercise meant not to create a poem but
to give us the experience of examining ourselves and our lives, with the
onion as our guide.

Within half an hour many of us were in tears, not from the onion but from
peeling away the protective layers we'd built around our lives that shielded
us from looking at ourselves honestly. This peeling away is an essential part
of writing a poem. The experience was not so different from digging in the
Indian grave, uncovering the layers of earth there. Albert Camus said, "A
man's work is nothing but this slow trek to rediscover, through the detours
of art, those two or three great and simple images in whose presence his
heart first opened." For me, one of these images is digging through the layers to get to the truth of something. It guides my work as a teacher of poetry
as well.

One of my first teaching sites in New York as a poet-in-residence was a school around 130th Street. As I approached the school I saw a blacktop surrounded by a tall wire fence. The tar was scattered with broken glass. It looked less like a school than like a prison.

I walked past the barred windows; the smell of garbage hung in the warm spring air. Inside, it was not much better. Many of the classrooms were overcrowded; in one room there were thirty-five first graders. But more than that conspired to make writing difficult: paper and crayons, scarce commodities, were kept in a locked closet.

How could anyone learn in this environment? How could anyone teach? Every day I felt despair threatening to overwhelm me. What could I possibly teach that would make a difference?

As time passed, I started to realize that while writing poetry couldn't solve these deep, systemic problems, it could help. It was the students who convinced me; the looks on their faces as they listened to poetry, what they said during the workshops, and most of all the poems they wrote pushed back my despair again and again. Sometimes it seemed as if the poems were islands of peace in a long war.

I was also able to peel away many of my own preconceptions about New York City. I began to look more closely. Instead of noticing only the garbage smell, broken bottles, and the bars on the windows, I began to notice empty lots turned into gardens, as well as many wonderful classrooms that were the inspiration for this book.

Carlos Fuentes once said, "Writing is a struggle against silence." In one sense, silence is the last thing you'll find in most schools; yet the silence that surrounds telling the truth and expressing emotion is pervasive. Poetry is one way to shatter this silence, and there are many classrooms that encourage it, but so often it's relegated to Columbus Day or Halloween or a single week in the spring. The opportunity for kids to learn the steady, constant expression of what's true for them is lost.

I've written *For the Good of the Earth and Sun* in the hope that this loss doesn't have to continue. I hope these chapters provide a place for the gradual peeling away of defenses that real learning requires. I also hope that the answers each of you finds at the end of that process are as diverse and resistant to conformity as the children and teachers I've had the privilege of working with these past six years.

1

Making Joy: Reading

Every writer of poetry is first a reader of poetry. I don't remember reading poems as a child, but I remember hearing them. My mother would recite "Pease porridge hot / Pease porridge cold / Pease porridge in the pot / Nine days old" or sing poem-songs like "Have you seen the muffin man, the muffin man, the muffin man. . . . " The nursery rhymes and poems were like friends to me. I'd walk around the house singing them over and over again and carried them wherever I went.

Recently, I gave a workshop to teachers on reading poetry and asked them to try to remember a poem they had read or heard when they were younger. Everyone could recite at least one. Some were old favorites like "Twinkle, Twinkle, Little Star," "Wynken, Blynken, and Nod," or " 'Twas the Night Before Christmas." When one started to recite, we would all join in.

When I read poetry to kindergartners and first graders, they sway and nod their heads and snap their fingers. I don't have to say, "Poetry is rhythmic, boys and girls; why don't you dance a little?" They know the music of the poem because they feel it in their bodies.

We all need to revive those old responses to poetry and trust them again. Does the poem make your body sway or break into dance? Does it make your insides move? Does it bring tears to your eyes, whether from grief or from joy? Reading or hearing a poem should feel like jumping into a cool lake in the summer or drinking a cold glass of water when you're thirsty. But most of our encounters with poetry have had the life squeezed out of them. We've been asked to memorize, analyze, write, and answer questions about poems we don't even choose to read. No wonder so many people come up to me and say, "I hate poetry." In order to want to talk about poetry, people must first like it. When I like a poem, my understanding of it has begun.

Once I came across Frost's "The Road Not Taken" in a textbook called, ironically, *Enjoying Literature*. I started reading the poem, enjoying its music, trying to understand it—then I noticed on the bottom of the page questions that students were supposed to answer. Some of the questions were:

- *Recalling*
  About what is the speaker sorry?
  What does the speaker doubt in lines 14–15?
  At the end of the poem, what does the speaker say "has made all the difference"?
- *Interpreting*
  Do you think the speaker feels he made the right choice? Why or why not?
- *Extending*
  What are some of the advantages and some of the disadvantages of not being able to reverse a decision?

Instead of being allowed to explore the poem through natural talk, curiosity, and revelation, students are forced to answer somebody else's questions, meant to help them "understand" the poem. With this introduction, it's no wonder that poetry isn't read in this country.

If I had to answer questions every time I read a poem, my enjoyment probably would change rapidly to resentment. The challenge of bringing the joy of reading poetry back into the classroom begins with *us*, as educators— if I'm afraid of exploring poetry, my students probably will be, too. I rescued my enjoyment of poetry when I began keeping a notebook to collect poems I loved. Sometimes I put in poems I remembered from when I was young. I also borrowed anthologies and poetry books from the library and searched them for poems I loved. I collected two types of poems: poems for my students and poems for me. Sometimes they were the same.

If I didn't like something, even if it was famous, I didn't include it. I looked for poems that had something to do with my life or that made me feel good or for poems from which I could learn about my own writing. I pasted poems I loved around my apartment—on the walls around my desk, in the bathroom—so that when I was at my desk or brushing my teeth before work, I could look up and read a poem. I put up poems that gave me the courage to live my life the way I want to live it.

But it takes time to be able to read poetry. As I was writing this book and teaching, I seldom had time to read. I was telling other people to read but not reading myself because I had to work, buy groceries, do the dishes, and so on. It was too easy to get bogged down in the chores of daily living; I needed to make time each week to sit down and read. Once I started, it got easier.

Reading poems can become part of a classroom's routine; you might read a poem a day or the same poem every day for a while. When it's time for math, a teacher could read Carl Sandburg's "Arithmetic"; at science time, I've read many poems on weather, animals, insects, and the natural world. Poems are written about so many subjects; it makes sense to integrate poetry into other parts of the day. Poetry can celebrate birthdays and holidays or reward achievement. But if it's relegated to "Poetry Week" in the spring, students see it as superfluous or insignificant. It should become as natural a part of their lives as play is.

When I'm choosing poems to read, I read poems I've written or students have written or favorites from books. I read poems whose inner life and language will permeate my students' world. I can see it on their faces when they're gathered around me, listening, taking in the cadences and the words, sometimes without even knowing it at first, the way a child hears a lullaby as she drifts into sleep. I read poems that will act as a key to open the doors to their feelings, their imaginations, and their voices.

Theodore Roethke says in "Open House":

> My secrets cry aloud
> I have no need for tongue.
> My heart keeps open house.
> My doors are widely swung.

Reading poems helps students keep open house. After hearing many poems, students begin to know what different kinds of poetry sound like, and they come to their own understanding of what makes a poem a poem. It's the equivalent of a young pianist hearing music from Chopin or Scott Joplin; our students' ears are being trained. They become familiar with the voice of poetry, which is crucial preparation for writing their own.

In a third-grade class I read some of Langston Hughes's poems, among them "April Rain Song." After I finished, one boy asked, "Why is that a poem? It doesn't rhyme."

I said, "I'm going to read the poem again. Let's all listen to it, and maybe you can tell me what you think."

I read the poem again, and the boy's hand shot up.

"He keeps saying the word 'rain' over and over . . . so it does kind of rhyme."

Other hands went up. One girl said, "It sounds like a song." Another said, "I could just picture the rain and hear it in my mind."

By listening a second time the kids were able to name some of the many different aspects of poetry: repetition, sound, rhythm, image. I didn't say, "This is a poem because . . . " They heard it for themselves, getting beyond the idea that all poems have to rhyme. It was a moment of discovery for them.

I've spent many hours with library books trying to find poems with powerful images as well as beautiful, compelling language, poems that reveal an experience, so that students can easily enter the poem's world, poems that rhyme and ones that don't, poems that tell a story, poems that are like songs. I look for poems as varied as trees or flowers or the many different faces on city streets—poems that tell the truth about the world, poems that will move my students. When I read them aloud in class, I read with the Native American belief that "words in themselves have the power to make things happen."

A colleague of mine, Ralph Fletcher, who is an excellent poet, sent a batch of his poems to an anthologist of children's poetry for possible publication. He received a rejection letter that began, "I like the poems, but remember this anthology is for grades K–4." Ralph had been reading these poems to kids for years, and they had loved them.

This is the trouble with a lot of children's poetry. So much is condescending or silly—as if this is the only kind of poetry children can like. There seems to be a real censorship.

I used to do the same thing, choosing only poems that I thought would be immediately accessible. But then I began to wonder. I like best poems I can keep returning to for more and more layers of understanding, not the ones I grasp immediately. There's nothing more exciting than the moment when the sense of a poem becomes clear; suddenly, meaning is unlocked. It's like fitting the last piece of a jigsaw puzzle in place.

When I worked with a class of fifth graders who'd been writing and reading poetry for a while, I brought a sheet of various poems to read and discuss. Almost unanimously they liked best the poems that were the more difficult to understand. The poems that were immediately accessible they compared to "grocery lists." They got bored with them easily.

Yet there's also a time and place for reading poems that students will understand immediately. Because children often don't like poetry or feel they can't understand it, it's important to give them first the success that comes with immediate comprehension. Later you can read poems that are more difficult and talk about ways to unfold them.

In the beginning I choose poems that I think will connect to my students' lives. In New York City, I've read not only poems about nature or everyday experience but also poems specifically about urban life. I try to include poems whose topics aren't stereotypically "poetic." Many students think poems can only be about love and flowers; I bring in poems about baseball, oil slicks, a grandmother, to help them see that poets write about anything in their lives. To start, I stay away from poems that have strong rhymes. This is the kind of poetry students already know; in fact, often it's the beginning and the end of what they think poetry is. Part of my job is to expand those boundaries.

I don't just pick poems that I think my students will like; I choose poems that I like, that I can share. If I read kids poems that don't interest me, it shows in my voice; I've had to take the time to search for words that satisfy us both. Many poems that weren't written with children in mind are wonderfully suited to the classroom. William Carlos Williams, Langston Hughes, Gwendolyn Brooks, Lucille Clifton, Anne Sexton, Theodore Roethke, and Elizabeth Bishop, just to name a few, have all written poems accessible to children as young as five.

Once the poem is chosen, the task of reading aloud remains. Here are a few tips I keep in mind when I'm reading poetry to students.

First, I respect the mood of the poem—somber and slow or light and playful, reflective or like a song. The mood will be echoed in the poem's rhythms, in its images, in the way it's shaped on the page and the way the lines are broken. I make sure I know what the mood is and read it with that in mind.

I read slowly enough for my students to piece together the images and the meaning. If I read too quickly, the poem will pass over them without connecting. On the other hand, if I read too slowly, the poem might seem fragmented, which might break the intended mood. I also respect the white space; when I see white space in a poem, it means silence—a visual and aural pause. The way the lines are broken and the way the poem is arranged on the page are a code the poet uses to indicate how the poem should be read.

I read a poem all the way through. I don't stop in the middle to explain a word or ask a question; it destroys the mood. At the end, I don't quiz my students or make them interpret the poem right away. I just let them sit with it for a while. Sometimes this may mean reading the poem twice or even three times. In the first reading, students just hear the poem. During the second, they become more familiar with the language and begin to piece together the meaning. One reading often goes by too quickly.

I read in as natural a voice as possible. I don't let my voice become monotonous, but I also try not to be overdramatic—if I'm too dramatic, I'll draw attention away from the poem to myself. I try to read with the voice that I think the poem dictates, to do justice to its mood and language. Sometimes it helps to pretend a friend is sitting next to me and I'm speaking the poem to this person. For me, this helps bring naturalness and intimacy to my voice.

Finally, I let my students see the poem I'm reading, either by giving them a copy or by copying the poem on large paper. Sometimes I read the poem first, then let them see it so that they can begin to study how a poem looks on the page.

I stagger into Debbie Futterman's third-grade class, lugging a big bag of books. I have visited Debbie's wonderful class before, and I know how enthusiastic her students are about reading. I spread the books out on tables and ask the students to choose what they want to read, either alone or in pairs. I've categorized the books into anthologies, thematic anthologies, and books by individual poets. I explain that on days when I know I'm going to write, I usually spend a couple of hours reading poems to get inspired.

The kids race to grab the book with the best cover or the best pictures. They spread out around the room, under tables, in corners. I show some of them my notebook, where I collect favorite lines, poems, feelings, and ideas that come to mind as I read. From the start, I've encouraged them to keep their own reading notebooks. Judging by the looks on their faces, you would think I'd just brought in a banquet.

As I walk with Debbie around the room, I notice two boys reading Myra Cohn Livingston's *Celebrations* (1985). They take turns reading it aloud to each other. I ask, "Why did you decide to read the poems aloud?"

"You can hear it," one boy says. "You read stories quietly and poems out loud."

The other boy says, "By reading it out loud you feel the meaning of the poem. You hear yourself saying a poem that somebody writes."

"What made you choose this book?" Debbie asks.

"Because I like books about special holidays." Nearby, Alicia is copying a poem into her notebook. When I ask her why, she says, "I like to read things to my mother. I want to read this poem to my mother, who doesn't know about poems."

Jenny has written "favorite lines" in a box in her journal, followed by the lines "He gives his harness bells a shake / To ask if there is some mistake," from "Stopping by Woods on a Snowy Evening." When I ask why she picked those lines, she answers, "I wrote them down because they rhyme, and because it gives me a picture without a picture."

Janice writes down names of her favorite poems from Carl Sandburg's *Early Moon* (1958). "Most of my favorite poems are quiet poems," she says.

"What do you mean by quiet?"

"If the poem's personality is quiet, calm, like the poem 'Sea Wash.' "

One group is preparing a choral reading of a poem they like. It's short, so they decide to memorize it and recite it to the class. A girl in the group says, "We want to show that if you really like a poem, you can memorize it."

Henry is sitting in a corner reading. He says about "Sea Wash," "It's like a river, like a washing machine that cleans things. It gives me a little feeling of something special."

I don't have to say too much. If the books are there, the children are eager to read and discover many ways to enjoy them. Sometimes I cancel the writing workshop and just spend a week or so reading. Other times I suggest they might want to spend the first half of the workshop reading and then move into writing when they're ready.

I also start off some workshops with choral reading. James Britton calls this "orchestrated reading"; the voices are like the different instruments. But in this case, there is no single conductor. The teacher isn't the conductor; the children are. As they look through the poems, they decide how to read, based on what the poem dictates. Is it soft? Does it ask for a soft solo voice or for a loud unison reading? Should each person read one line at a time or two lines at a time, or perhaps parts of a line because of the repeating pattern? Do the rhythms vary? Should the voices reflect that variation?

The students in one class in Brooklyn got into groups of three or four, and each group chose a poem to read aloud. Some chose "No Matter," by Lee

Bennett Hopkins; others chose Nikki Giovanni's "Knoxville, Tennessee." After a twenty-minute discussion and practice time, they were ready. Each performance was beautiful and unique; afterward, we discussed why each group had decided to read the poems as they did.

Sometimes I give all my students the same poem to choral read, and we learn from the different interpretations. Sometimes they choose a favorite poem themselves. To begin they often read the poem the first way that occurs to them; I nudge them to try two or three different ways before choosing the best. Later, as they read and write more poetry, their readings and interpretations become more sophisticated.

For many students who are afraid of or bored with poetry, choral readings offer a way to get to know a poem more intimately and to establish a relationship with poetry. Students begin to read and reread poetry, to live with a poem beyond the initial reading, and to share reading poetry with their friends.

Stanley Kunitz wrote:

> Above all, poetry is intended for the ear. It must be felt to be understood, and before it can be felt, it must be heard. Poets listen for their poems, and we, as readers, must listen in turn. If we listen hard enough, who knows—we too may break into dance, perhaps for grief, perhaps for joy.

Once I saw a bumper sticker that read, "Don't postpone joy." This motto should guide anyone who is beginning to learn about poetry, whatever the grade level. The reading and writing of poetry must begin with the joy of it.

2
"Here Is the Deep Water": How to Begin

Before I taught poetry in New York City, I spent a year in New Hampshire as poet-in-residence at a small school at the foot of the White Mountains. A few days before I was to begin, I sat in a big armchair in front of a wood stove, surrounded by books on the teaching of poetry. After I'd read them, the question remained: How to begin? According to the books, I could ask students to pretend that their poems would be buried in space capsules and survive the destruction of the earth and to write a poem about what it would be like for someone to unearth them, or to write a poem beginning with "I wish," or to write from the point of view of a falling leaf, in haiku or cinquain, or to pretend to be a window in the World Trade Center and write a poem about that. I stared into the fire, thinking about these ideas. Why didn't they work for me? Partly it was because I'd already been influenced by the ideas of Lucy Calkins and others on the teaching of writing. And partly it was because I knew I wouldn't want to write about any of those things. Why would I? My poems begin with a feeling—something I care deeply about—and none of these ideas involved anything I really cared about.

Once I decided the books wouldn't work for me, I began to look to myself. I was a poet. I had written many poems. What was, for me, the essence of poetry? Maybe if I could distill this, I could bring it to students. I started writing frantically in my notebook.

"Many of my poems begin with a feeling, some deep urge. Sometimes it's so strong I actually feel something inside me move. It can happen any time; it happens about ideas, memories, things I see every day. Often I start with an image, a picture in my mind. I use this as a resource to guide me in the making of the rest of the poem." As I wrote, my tired, going-to-sleep body beside the fire started coming to life. I felt excited about talking to my students about poetry.

A few days later I drove up Route 93 to a small school in Campton; the snowy White Mountains were in full view as I exited the highway. I drove down a country road and over a small bridge to the school where nine grades were taught.

The first classroom I visited that day was a kindergarten; I was starting with the lower grades, then would slowly move up and finish with the eighth. I was so nervous that I asked the teacher to leave for the first fifteen minutes, so I could be more myself. Once she was safely out the door, I gathered the students on a rug and talked to them about making poems. The kids' faces were so small; they were so young. I'd never worked with kindergarten kids before. I told them exactly what was essential for me to make a poem.

"All my poems start with a strong feeling I have about something," I said. "Then usually I try and get a picture of it in my mind. Let me give you an example. This summer a bat got into my house. I walked across the living room, and all of a sudden this huge . . . what looked like a shadow . . . came flying toward me."

Excitement leaped into their faces. Hands started going up. "I've seen a bat." "One time a bat got into my house. . . . " They all wanted to talk about bats. I listened to their stories, then continued.

"I was so afraid, I ran into the kitchen and hid in a corner. Then a friend of mine hit the bat with a broom and got it into a box to let it outside. I remember how it crawled out of the box. It was only about as big as a mouse. And it kind of turned around and looked at me as it was crawling on the stone wall. What was I afraid of? I felt sorry for it. The picture of the bat will never leave my mind. Here's the poem I wrote to share with you."

The Bat

I stood in the doorway
watching a bat circle the room.
Its wings sounded like a cloth
shaken out of a window.

It flew into the lighted kitchen
where we captured it
in a cardboard box.
We let it out the door
and it hobbled across a rock
its wings dragging behind it.
Then it turned its small bat face towards me
its body no larger than a mouse
and it disappeared into the night.

They all looked as though they were trying to picture it.

"That's something that happened to me, that I wrote about. Why don't you all close your eyes and think about what's important to *you*—something that's happened to you, something you care about, anything." I could see them all thinking.

"Okay," I said, "does someone want to share what they saw in their minds?"

Laura raised her hand. "All I see are stars," she said. "Stars, stars everywhere. They look like they're brand new. Sometimes when I look at stars I get afraid. Stars. Stars everywhere."

What she said sounded like a poem, and I told her so; as more kids told about their ideas, what they said sounded like poetry also. I was surprised, and delighted.

"Why don't you go back to your seats and draw a picture of what you saw? Then try to make the poems the best you can."

Here are some of the poems they wrote. Most used invented spelling, some just marks that resembled letters; I preferred that they try to write on their own. All of them told their poems verbally first and later were able to remember the exact wording if asked to repeat them.

I was amazed by that first day, by how powerful the poems were. Katrina wrote and said:

Here is a ship
That's sailing on the water.
I'm going to put a sun in it.
The sun gets stuck
and it's shaped like a moon.
Then it darkens like a moon.
It is a moon.

A great example of metaphor.
William wrote:

> These are moons
> all of these moons.
> I've seen too many moons.

I'll never forget Seth, who, when I walked up and asked if he could say his poem to me, began,

> Once there was a storm
> and all the gold was getting all wet
> and was going to blow.
> All boats, houses were going to blow up.
> All the wind and water.
> The bat, he was mad
> So he pushed the water
> and he took it
> and he took the water . . .

"Seth," I said to him. "That's quite a poem." It was like interrupting Shakespeare. He looked at me impatiently, then continued:

> Then the bat made the water go so fast . . .

He could have gone on like that, a kindergarten Shakespeare, all day long. I think I had beginner's luck.

But not all first days work out that beautifully. Toward the end of that year, I worked in the eighth grade. I was introduced to the students as Georgia Heard The Poet, who would be working with them on their own poems. Half the class stared to giggle; some said, "Oh, no," and rolled their eyes. At first, I felt a little hurt—was it me? Why didn't they like me? I took a deep breath and began. (By then I'd gained enough confidence to allow the teacher to stay in the room.)

"When I walked in, I noticed a lot of people groaned and said, 'Oh, no.' I don't think it's because of me. I think it's because I'm talking about poetry. So, let's talk about poetry, to clear the air. How many people here don't like poetry?"

Half the class raised their hands.

"How many *do* like it?"

A few hands.

"Okay, let's talk about it. A question for those of you who really don't like it: Why not?"

A few hesitant hands went up. I knew what they were thinking: "Is she serious?" One boy said, "It's boring." He got a lot of "yeahs" for that one.

Somebody else said, "It's about boring things like flowers and love—mushy things."

I got the message.

"I wouldn't be a poet if poetry were only those things," I told them, "boring, too hard, only about mushy subjects. And I've been doing this a long time. Sure, sometimes I read bad poetry. But poetry can be exciting; it can be about baseball or guitar players or anything else you want it to be about." The antipoetry faction looked unconvinced; but within a week some of the most reluctant had become the stars of the class, the ones for whom poetry was working. One boy who was adamantly against poetry that first day wrote one of the class's most moving poems:

I Think This Is Where My Real Father Lives

I think this is where
my real father lives. It's near
a river. I see a light
in one of the rooms.

Someone is pulling
up the driveway with a car.
The chimney is smoking.
I see an oak tree
in the back yard.
As I get farther and
farther away, I see a shadow
in the distance, now gone.

I've taught and learned in scores of schools since that first residency; but some of the things I've come to believe are crucial to teaching poetry I found the first day in that kindergarten. Chris was quiet, and I barely remember his face, but he wrote one of the most profound poems in the class:

Here is the deep water.

I showed this to a friend of mind, a poet, who thought it such a powerful metaphor for life that she put a copy above her desk. Those five-year-old kids knew so much about poetry; their work was full of emotions, images, rhythm, beautiful sounds. Most of all, it was full of what was on their minds and in their hearts, full of their authentic, inimitable voices.

That beginning encouraged me to try various other beginnings, some very different but all of which owe something to the essentials I learned there:

- It helps for a teacher to ask the whole class to set aside other projects for a while and focus on poetry.
- The use of the image, the picture in the mind, is one useful way to help students begin to write poems.
- Poems come from something deeply felt; it's essential for student poets to be able to choose their own topics according to what's important to them.

After my residency in New Hampshire I moved back to New York to teach teachers and kids in the city through the Teachers College Writing Project. Those first teaching experiences helped me develop some strategies in a calm, small-school environment, but the years that followed challenged and encouraged my ideas over and over again.

It's a cold morning in December when I walk into the large brick school building. Hot, dry air blasts from the radiator. As I enter the building I notice an entire wall covered with snow poems, all written on paper cut into snow-flake shapes. I stop to read a few. They all go something like this: "Snow is nice. Snow is white. I like snow." They are all written on the same white, lined paper, in what looks like the same handwriting, with the same titles, all spelled perfectly.

Something in me panics when I see such sameness in writing. For me it represents the death of what poetry is all about: individual expression, variety, seeing the universal in the particular. Many people don't believe children have their own ideas, their own lives to express. After a while chil-dren begin to believe this is true.

Walking through the double doors I pass a woman sitting behind a school desk, who stops me and asks where I'm going. "To the general office," I say. She asks me to sign a sheet, hands me an official white school pass, and directs me up the stairs.

In the office I notice several mothers leaning against the counter, waiting. One secretary is on the phone, the other walking around with papers in her hand. A small girl with glasses, whose feet barely reach the edge of the bench, sits and cries. No one notices her. I take the visitors' book from the counter to sign; the time clock where teachers punch in and out is behind me. I sign a big leatherbound book whose first entry dates from the 1920s. After greeting the principal I walk to my first class.

It's a fourth grade, right next door to the office. The teacher, Mrs. Blum, sits at her desk. She is a large woman who looks up over her glasses when I come in, greets me warmly, and tells the class to be quiet. I immediately notice the atmosphere; bars are on the windows, striping the view onto row houses. The bulletin board is covered with dittoed sheets of spelling tests and good work in the usual handwriting, with "Excellent" written on them. The room is more welcoming than many other classrooms I've been in; Thanksgiving mobiles hang from the lights, and there's a shelf full of books. There isn't the air of sterility I usually encounter. I watch the kids watching me as I walk to the front of the room. I introduce myself to Mrs. Blum before asking the kids to come to the front and sit on the floor.

There are thirty-two of them; it's crowded. I wait until they seem settled.

"Hello. My name is Georgia Heard, and I'm a poet," I say. "I'm here to talk to you about poetry and about writing poems. Before I start, I just want to ask you a few questions about what you think poetry is. What makes a poem a poem? Any ideas?"

Philip is tiny and fragile-looking. He has an old, wise face, like a miniature of an adult's. I immediately like him. "All poems rhyme," he says.

"No. Not all of them," says Peter, who is sitting next to him.

"You're both right," I say. "Sometimes poems rhyme, and sometimes they don't. If they don't rhyme, then what makes them a poem?"

Peter has thick glasses that magnify his eyes. His speech is a little slow. He looks like he's thinking. "They're usually short and funny," he says.

"Yes, a lot of times they're shorter than stories. Sometimes they're like Shel Silverstein's poems. But not all of them I read or write are funny. But sometimes they're like Shel Silverstein's poems." They all nod and exclaim with recognition.

Natasha has a wide, round face, her hair pulled back in a short ponytail with a wide barrette. "The way I think of poems sometimes," she says, "is like songs with no music."

It always moves me when kids leave the stereotype of what they've been taught about poetry and come up with their own definitions. " 'Songs with no music,' " I say. "That sounds like a great way to describe a poem." I let that one sink into me.

Kasey, wearing a white sweatshirt emblazoned with one word in black that I don't understand and looking a little angry, says, "I think poems are boring." A few boys around him giggle at his brave pronouncement.

I love this kind of defiance; he's saying what he really feels. "Sometimes you're right," I say. "Sometimes I read poems in magazines and I think they're boring, too. But that's not all. Sometimes the poems I read are wonderful and exciting and not just about boring subjects. Maybe we can find you some poems that won't be boring."

So many poems I read when I was young seemed to have nothing to do with my life. Sometimes it wasn't the poems that made me feel that way, but the teachers. If I didn't understand, I felt there was something wrong with me. Many teachers have had similar experiences with poetry. No wonder poetry is boring to kids.

I gather from this class's comments that they haven't had too much experience with poetry—except maybe a little with a certain kind of rhyming, funny poetry, like Shel Silverstein's.

"For me, all poetry comes from a feeling I have about something," I say. "Everybody has feelings. Sometimes I'm happy, sad, angry, frustrated, worried, whatever it is. Sometimes I'm walking down the street or driving, and I'll see something or remember something that I feel so strongly it makes my insides move. Then I know there's a possibility for a poem there.

"But you can't just write, 'I am sad, I am sad, I am sad.' That wouldn't make a poem. So sometimes I try to get an image in my mind, a picture in my mind of what makes me feel this feeling. Let me give you an example.

"I was sitting in my room one day feeling sad about my grandfather, who died years ago. I was remembering summers I used to spend with him. I got out paper, and this picture came to my mind of a time when I went to the woods to dig in this Indian grave my grandfather told me about. I just wrote down the image and then let whatever else, whatever other images, come into my mind, not worrying about spelling or if it was a good poem yet. I just kept writing my feelings and the image on paper. This is what the first draft looked like." (See Figure 2–1.)

"It looks kind of like a story," says one girl.

"A lot of my poems start out like stories," I say, "but then I cut and craft the poem.

"In my first draft it wasn't clear to me what I wanted to say, what the poem was about, or what the poem would look like when it was finished. I just wrote, making a collage of words, not knowing which parts might eventu-

```
I went out to see the Indian grave
that my grandfather told me about
at the edge of the woods near the burning field.
I removed the leaves and stones that covered the mound
and I dug all afternoon until the woods
got dark and I saw the kitchen light of the house
in back of me go on.
What ever it was that I didn't find frightened me.
It is the same thing that I heard in the whiporwill's voice
coming out of the dark woods that sounded like a whinnying horse
or like an animal that was lost or abandoned or teasing me.
I don't know what it is.
It has something to do with my dead grandfather
and the pictures I have of him walking around in my head
in the Oldfield's house.
Something about his absence that eludes my grasp
that I can't even speak about.
I'm trying to capture something that's not even there.
Something about the room where my grandfather walks
where he appears or disappears in my head
or the way his clocks still ring —
sound differently without him around.
As if they are ticking and chiming like the way light
or a single day differs.  It sounds like they miss him
like they are empty without him.
The whole house feels this way.
Or like his words the way they aren't even words anymore
but just memory of an action of trying to unbury the
Indian grave where we didn't find a thing and knew we
wouldn't but we found a loniliness later on in life
that is equal to the nothingness we found in the Indian grave,
equal to the meaning that keeps eluding our grasp,
to the whiporwill's cry, equal to how frightening
or why the forest frightens at night, equal to any fear.
```

Figure 2–1   A first draft

ally stay. It felt more like journal writing. I tried not to censor any images or thoughts; I needed to find out what the poem had to tell me. I had to step out of its way and let it speak for itself.

"My next draft looks like this. [See Figure 2–2.] I kept all the strong images, cut away what I didn't think belonged, typed up the poem, and said 'I'm finished.' When I read it again a few days later I got the feeling it wasn't right. I measured what I had down on paper against what I had in my heart and knew my poem wasn't finished. I knew I had to go back to the first-draft stage.

"Once I'd returned to the feeling that started the poem and tried to 're-vision' it, new images came to mind. I wrote these down. [See Figure 2–3.]

```
Oldfields

I went out to see the Indian grave
my grandfather told me about
at the edge of the woods, near the burning-field.

I removed the leaves and stones
that covered the mound, and dug all afternoon
until the woods got dark,
and the kitchen light of the house
in back of me came on.

Except for the dirt
that sifted through my hands,
the grave was empty.


My dead grandfather walks around the rooms
of the empty summer house.

All day his clocks, behind him on the mantel,
have been ticking in my head.
```

Figure 2–2   A second draft

"Then, when I felt all the material was there, I started to craft the lines and take out words and choose better ones. The later drafts were a process of 're-visioning' the experience, adding new material to the collage. As if I were working with clay, I molded it slowly, fine-tuning it in the process, trusting when I felt it wasn't quite finished, savoring the heart-pounding feeling that came when I wrote almost exactly what I felt inside. [See Figure 2–4.]

"In the final draft I divided the poem into four sections, based on the four different images I saw." (See p. xviii–xix.) I tell the kids I'm going to read it to them.

After I've finished, a boy says, "It sounds like a story." Others say, "It doesn't rhyme," "I saw your grandfather walking around in the house," "I get a lonely feeling." I told them, "Even as I read it now, I realize I need to write another poem about this. I still have more to say."

I suggest that it's time for them to consider what they might write about. We sit together in quiet for a few minutes. Some kids have their eyes closed.

```
I am standing near the wall
at the edge of the turning field
and I can see my grandfather
walk through the dining room
of the empty summer house.
He is ten years dead
he is whitish, thin like air,
his head is looking down
near the window.

In the living room his large grandfather
clock is ticking,
ever hour it will break into chimes.

Up the back staircase
in my bedroom I lie  awake
as a child unable to sleep,
tossing and turning
the unfamiliar smell of the sheets
that smell like pine.
I am hot and I toss and turn
afraid of having the clock strike
midnight.  Every one else in bed
asleep Id I can hear the clock
ticking and ringing preparing
and getti g ready by the short chimes
for the one long chime at midnight.
I am afraid that the chime of the clock
will let the spirits out into the room
that somehow this is their meeting time
downstairs in the dark living room.
And that after grandfather died
he will be among xu them.
And I can see the spirits fly out
like smoke going through a fan
but they are black into the room
They are evil and I am afraid
that they are going to hurt me.
```

Figure 2–3   New images

Some exclaim an excited, "I got it!" After a few minutes I ask them to whisper their ideas to the person beside them. I hear "my grandmother who died," "my dog," "stars," "the seasons," a whole range of ideas. I think of the snowflake poems and of how different these ideas are.

At first, some students don't believe they really can write poems about their own lives. Often they tell me nothing is very important to them; they pick traditionally poetic topics like stars or seasons. But the more they hear of what I and other poets write about, the more they believe they can write

```
Oldfields


I went out to see the Indian grave
at the edge of the woods
near the burning field.

I picked off the leaves and stones
and dug all afternoon
until the woods grew dark
and the kitchen light of the house
behind me came on.

I expected to find jewels,
pots and arrows
or an Indian headress
with feathers in it.

Except for the dirt
that filtered through my hands,
the grave was empty.


I am standing near the wall
at the edge of the burning field.
I see you walk around t;he rooms
around the rooms
of the empty summer house.
Hunched over, thin as air
You have been dead for years
you walk a          path from the kitchen
through the dining room.

Years ago
up the front staircase
in my bedroom in this summer house
I lay in bed awake
listening for the clock
downstairs to strike midnight.
I see the spirits fly out of the clock
like black smoke going up a fan.

In the living room
      grandfather clock
is still ticking

Any hour now,
it will break into          chime.
```

Figure 2–4   A later draft

not only about nature but about a birthday party, an aunt who died, the shape of the earth, being scared.

I remind them not to worry right away about spelling or punctuation or about if it's a great poem, just to get their thoughts and feelings down. I want them to know that I write my first drafts with only the good angel on my shoulder, the voice that approves everything I write. This voice doesn't ask me questions like, "Is this any good? Is this a poem? Are you a poet?" I keep that other voice at a distance, letting only the good angel keep whispering to me: trust yourself, your feelings, your images; you can't worry the poem into existence. Later, the critical voice will be helpful to the poem, and over the years I've learned to acknowledge the critical side as I write, to let the voices converse as amiable equals. But for beginning poets the censoring voice, the voice that forbids risk and revelation, is louder than the whispers of the good angel, who knows they can pull the poem off.

They look eager to go back and write. I remind them again: "Most poets don't finish their poems in one day. First I write my thoughts; then I usually reread again and again, closing my eyes, looking in my mind to see if what's on the paper matches what's in my heart. If it's not right, I go back and try again."

Navine asks, "Does it have to rhyme?"

"No. You can rhyme your poems if you want; but let me warn you that sometimes rhyming makes you say things you don't really want to say. Things that don't make sense. Keep that in mind."

Somebody else asks, "Do you have to begin with a title?"

"The title usually comes last for me," I say. "Sometimes I don't even know what the poem's about. I have to discover that as I write. I think of titles after I finish. But then again some poets start with titles. That's up to you."

Some kids write sitting on the floor or on the rug, in different corners of the room. I ask Mrs. Blum how much exposure to poetry the kids have had. "Not much this year," she says. "We started with stories. Although we did read some Silverstein together." I stand with her at the edge of the room, looking around until everyone has chosen paper and settled down. A few girls have moved their seats and write together at a round table in the back. Many have started immediately. Some stare straight ahead, either still deciding what to write about or debating how they will say it.

Sometimes I think that the information about how to write a poem is less important than the atmosphere of the room. There are places that give me an excited urge to write, places that feel rich and warm, where time slows down and whatever I want to do is possible. For me, it might be a Sunday afternoon browsing in a Village bookstore, the sound of classical music in the background. For a little while, routine is suspended; I drift from thought to thought and feel happy to be alive. Sometimes when I was a girl my mother would cook a turkey on Sunday; the smells permeated the house as I lay upstairs on my bed reading and gave me the same feeling of peace. It's important that classrooms have this richness: books standing on the table,

Figure 2–5 "Short Times"

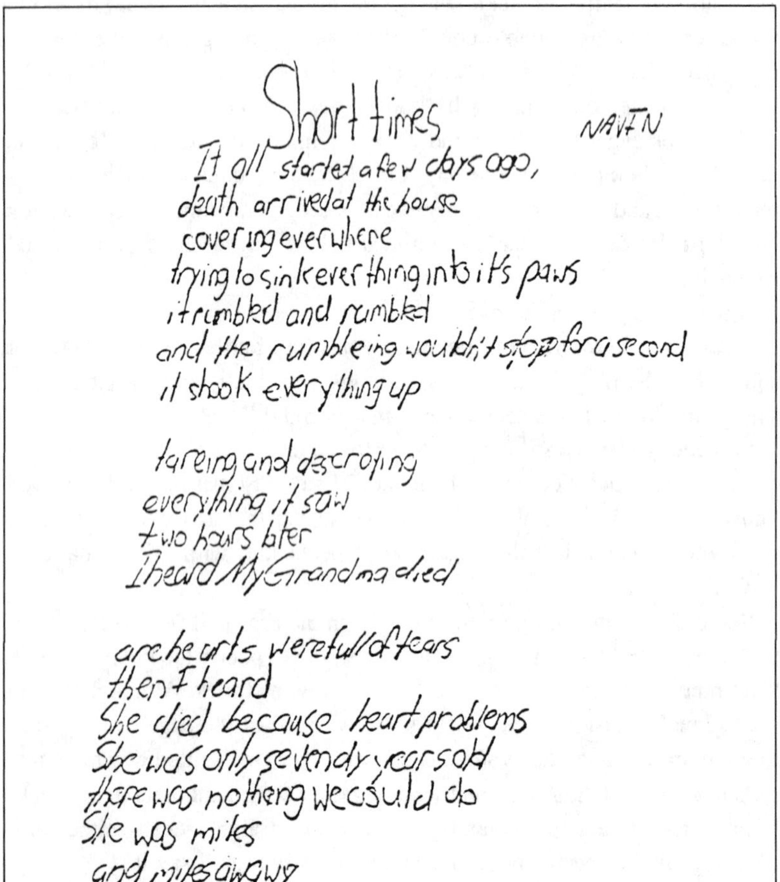

Short times
NAVIN

It all starled a few days ago,
death arrivedat the house
coveringeverwhere
trying to sinkeverthing intoit's paws
itrumbled and rumbled
and the rumbleing woulden't stop fora second
it shook everythingup

tareing and destroying
everything it saw
two hours later
IheardMyGrandma died

are hearts werefullof tears
then I heard
She died because heartproblems
She was only sevendy years old
there was nothing we could do
She was miles
and milesawawy

poems on large paper displayed all over, quotes by poets on the walls, kids writing everywhere, intently.

Where teachers and students have collaborated to create such richness, the kids' poems are filled with it, as shown in Figures 2–5 through 2–9.

It's a chilly March morning on the Cross Bronx Expressway; the air is filled with soot glowing like mist in a spotlight from the sun shining between overpasses and the lights of all the cars and trucks. I exit at Webster Avenue and pass boarded-up gas stations, empty lots, gutted buildings. Down a few side roads is the school, across the street from a park on one side and two burned buildings on the other; it looks modern.

Figure 2–6 "Atlantis" by Alex

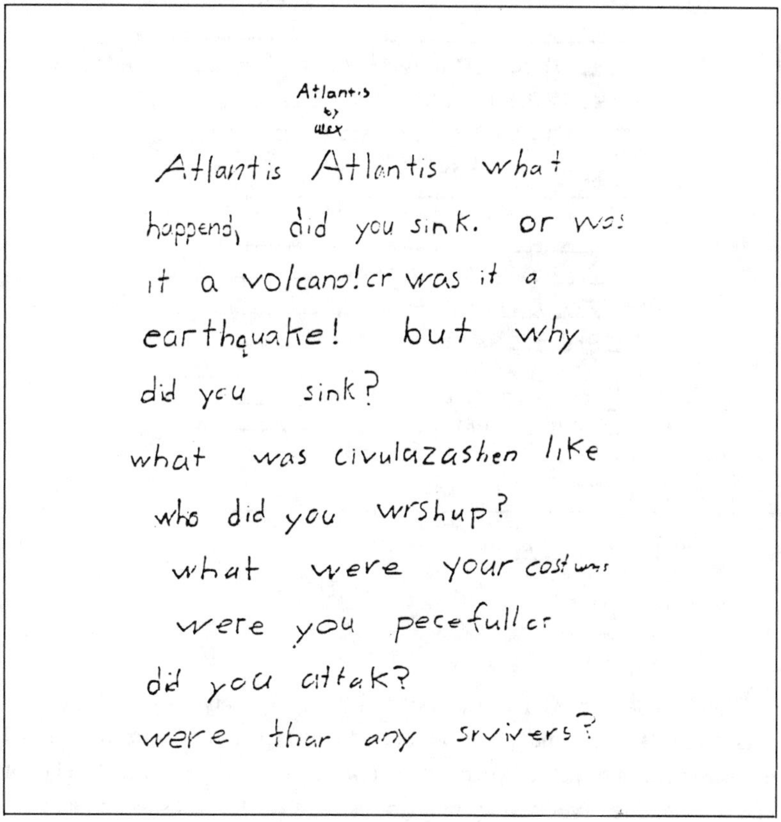

Atlantis
by
alex

Atlantis Atlantis what happend, did you sink. or was it a volcano! or was it a earthquake! but why did you sink?

what was civulazashen like who did you wrshup?
what were your costums
were you pecefull or
did you attak?
were thar any srvivers?

Figure 2–7 *"Long Ago on Earth"*

Clutching a canvas bag of books, I find my way to a second-floor classroom. It's a second grade taught by Joan Backer, who's been involved in the Writing Project for years and is one of the most dedicated teachers I know. The kids have been writing stories for a while, and she wants to get them started on poetry.

We say wolves

We say wovles are big.
Who said that?
We say wovles are bad.
Who said that?
And we say wovles howl at
the moon.
who said that?
They can be howling at the
dogstar.

Figure 2–8   "We Say Wolves"

Figure 2–9   "Sad Eyes" by Donald

Sad Eyes

My dog was laying on the
hard ground in the sun.
I went out and look at
him. He looked at me
with his sad eyes.
It seen like he was
saying can I come
inside.

The crowded classroom feels warm and alive. I ask the kids to come sit in a small space on the floor, near the blackboard. Although I often begin the poetry workshop using drafts of poems, as I described before, there are many different ways to begin; today I want to read them some of my favorite poems. Most of the children are looking right at me, curious, interested. Some are in dresses and crisp pants, others in clothes that show wear and age; all of them have that vivid life in their faces that in second grade is still very much present.

I introduce myself and say I'm going to read a few poems. The first is by Langston Hughes. "It's called 'April Rain Song,' " I tell them. A few kids "ooh" at the mention of his name.

"Let the rain kiss you." I hear a few giggles. "Let the rain beat upon your head with silver liquid drops."

April Rain Song

Let the rain kiss you.
Let the rain beat upon your head with silver liquid drops.
Let the rain sing you a lullaby.

The rain makes still pools on the sidewalk.
The rain making running pools in the gutter.
The rain plays a little sleep-song on our roof at night—

And I love the rain.

After I finish, they say, "I heard the rain." "I saw the rain kissing people." Everyone laughs.

"That's one of my favorite lines," I say. " 'Let the rain kiss you.' It was such a surprise to me; instead of saying 'Let the rain fall on you,' which wouldn't have been as interesting, he said, 'Let the rain kiss you.' "

"What does it mean?" Yolanda asks.

"Everyone, close your eyes," I say. "Imagine walking outside. It's a spring morning, and the rain is falling very, very softly. You tip your face up; imagine that it falls on your face, your cheeks. Do you feel it? Doesn't it feel like light kisses all over your face?"

They all giggle again. Some shout "No!" "This is another thing poets do," I say, "make you feel things so well. Can't you just picture it?

"I'm going to read another one," I tell them. "This is one of my favorites: 'Things,' by Eloise Greenfield, from a book called *Honey, I Love.*"

Things
Went to the corner
Walked in the store
Bought me some candy
Ain't got it no more
Ain't got it no more

Went to the beach
Played on the shore
Built me a sandhouse
Ain't got it no more
Ain't got it no more

Went to the kitchen
Lay down on the floor
Made me a poem
Still got it
Still got it

As I read, a group of girls sitting cross-legged in the back snap their fingers, heads and bodies moving with the rhythm of the poem. "This poet describes how I feel about poems all the time," I say. "And I loved the way some of you were snapping your fingers. That's another thing about poems; a lot of times they make your fingers want to snap, because they have a beat."

"Will you read it again?"

"If some of you want to get together and try reading poems as a group, you might do that."

Later, the group of girls who had been snapping stand at the front of the class, two speaking in unison the refrain, the other two the lines, all snapping their fingers and moving from side to side.

"Why don't you take a few minutes and think over what you might write about?" Everyone sits in silence, some with eyes closed, some not.

After a minute, some share their ideas. Joan has created a real feeling of trust in the class: they plan to write about apartment fires where they lost everything, one about a grandfather who shook a knife at a dog and was shot and killed by police, one about living with grandparents. Some plan to write about flowers, some about snow, one about seasons, one about July fourth in the city. Joan has read to them so much that the first day isn't as crucial as it might have been if they'd never heard poetry before. It's only a small step from that kind of immersion to writing poems of their own.

Most of the kids start to write. Nia comes up and says, "I have an idea, but I'm not sure how I should begin."

"What's the first thing that comes into your mind?"

"I see—"

"No, don't tell me," I say. "Just write it down, and I'll be around in a second."

Joan says, "A few kids are saying, 'I don't know what to write about.' What do I do?"

"That happens to poets all the time," I say. First, I suggest lots of possible topics to those who are struggling; not specific things like a pinball machine or a brother, but the big issues: something they're worried about, excited about, concerned about, knowledgeable about, feelings they've had, things they've seen that they can't forget, things they've heard on the news or though a friend, seen in the paper, family, memories, questions about the world. Sometimes just letting students know that poets can write about anything helps them think of an idea. As I speak, usually a few minds spark, and their owners stand up to go write.

For others, I offer a few strategies. Here are examples:

- Sit for a while with your eyes closed and see if anything comes to mind.
- Read some poetry; sometimes reading gets me excited about writing. Or look through an anthology's table of contents to see what other poets have written.
- Walk around to see what other people are writing about.
- Look through some of your stories to see if there's any poem material there.
- Walk to the window and look outside; take your paper and see if there's anything interesting out there. Sometimes just leaving a table where everyone is writing furiously is enough to bring out some ideas.
- Try free-writing; just put your pencil on the paper and write, no matter what, just to see what comes out. Even if at first it's only, "I'm sitting here—I don't know what to write about," sometimes just having words down will bring other words.

In many classes I've worked in, students have decided to try some of these ideas. In one first grade, Matthew decided to stand on a chair looking out the window at all the rooftops in Brooklyn; then he wrote about what he saw. (See Figure 2–10.)

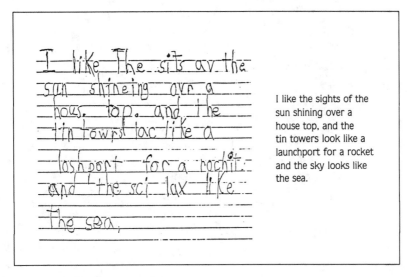

I like the sights of the sun shining over a house top, and the tin towers look like a launchport for a rocket and the sky looks like the sea.

Figure 2–10   What Matthew saw

In a third grade in the South Bronx, Deone chose to begin with free-writing; I watched her put pencil to paper and fill two full pages. When she finished, it sounded so much like a stream-of-consciousness poem that she decided to keep it as it was. (See Figure 2–11.)

Free-writing doesn't always end up as poetry; sometimes it just helps unblock your mind, as it did for Christine in Figure 2–12. It was only later in the writing that what was really on her mind emerged.

Two boys in a corner are reading; I ask them about what poems they like. They protest having to write poetry. Alejandro says, "I don't want to write poetry. When you're writing a story you can have more adventure. Poems can have adventure, but not that much. It can have some, but for me poems are calm, and I like to write about adventure."

Chopin says, "I like adventure, too, and poetry isn't that long."

"Anyway," says his friend, "I'm used to writing stories, and poems can't be scary, gross, or anything else."

I tell them about a long adventure poem called "The Odyssey" and promise to bring in some scary poems. They don't look convinced. But I know not to give up; some of the most poetry-hostile students turn out to be the most excited and inspired poets.

"Since you both like adventure, why don't you write an adventure poem?" I ask.

The sun came out and melted everybody and melted everything Even the building and melted the trees and the grass and the cars, trucks, Buses, vans, bike horses, cows, Pigs, dogs, caty monKeys/Kanels Even the Farms and Even it melted it self too and the ground and Windows and the clouds Fell down and then melted them and they turned gray and the sky turned black and the insects died and blood was all over the world and God came down and moped all of it up and he saw a lot of bones and he went back home and got some fruits and throw them down to the ground and people came out and some people came the fruit but they wasn't people they were bones of people and people Worms and then Books and then blood and then ants and then cereal and then a head and the soup and then grass and then numbers and then the ground and then tree and then a lot of house and then sand and then gold and then crayons and then fruit and then clothes and the stores and then animals and the water and then Fire works and then toys... and then things you eat with and then Plants and then flowers and no more insects and then balls and then hair and then skin mops and then pencils and pens and then leaves and then it start to rain and When it stoped raining it started to snow a lot and then letters.

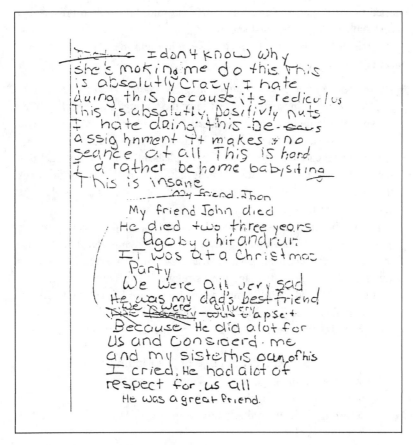

Figure 2–12 Christine's free-writing

The boys crinkle their noses.

"Okay, I'll tell you what. You can keep reading today; for next time I'll bring in some adventure poems, and you two can be thinking of how to write your own. Okay?"

They nod.

Sometimes it takes them a little while to get their feet wet. Reading poems is one of the best ways. One boy in Brooklyn said to me, "Poetry and spelling are my worst subjects. I'm only good at writing dialogue—and poems don't have dialogue." I always carry a poetry anthology; the one I had that day happened to contain some poems by Robert Frost. When I showed the boy poems with dialogue, like "Death of a Hired Man," he was convinced and started to write. Later he came up to me and said, "Poetry isn't one of my worst subjects anymore. Just spelling."

No matter how I decide to begin, I keep in mind these lessons my own writing has taught me:

• *Poems start with a feeling, and an image is one powerful way to convey feeling.* Which comes first, the image or the feeling? For me, they often arrive at the same time. Last summer I flew to Colorado with some colleagues to give a summer workshop. I taught a writing section for teachers, who were taken by surprise—some not pleasantly so—by the fact that they had to write. At first they almost mutinied; by the end of the week they were so involved in their writing that they were staying after the sessions to write, even on warm June afternoons

During the week, I visited Rocky Mountain National Park; we drove up to where we could stand on a ledge and see mountain after mountain for miles. The next day I sat down to write a poem, inspired by how moved I was by the teachers' fear and their struggle to explore their own lives. As I wrote, I found myself remembering how alone I felt in the middle of the mountains, even with other humans nearby. The combination of these feelings and the image of the mountain compelled me to write the poem.

We Stand at the Edge of the Mountain

We stand at the edge of the mountain
at the alpine tundra
where trees grow bald and then stop.
A hill of rocks,
mustard and green lichen—the mountain's only survivors.
Down below in the valley
a river winds, loops over green boulders
scattered everywhere in the alluvial fan.
Snow-capped mountains blue in the haze.
Clouds move across molten rock. The wind cries.

We stand at the edge of the mountain
darkness swells over us,
air turns greyer, icier.
We are certain only of a few things:
full moon rising over the tundra,
mountains deepening behind us,
stars icy and still.

What reason to trust
standing at the edge of this cliff,
stumbling in arctic wind,
climbing this far up alone?
What reason to think that anything
can survive here?
Temperature falling to zero at night.
Plants hundreds of years old
only a few inches high,
root themselves into the earth
seeking shelter even in snow.

As a poet, I try to explore experience in as much depth as I can; I often use the image as my guide. It roots emotion to the concrete, to the world, so the poem is not too vague or abstract. It's not simply a "picture in your mind"; it's the thin, dry skin on my grandfather's hands, the rain on Langston Hughes's face, the place where the mountains and the courage of those teachers meet.

• *Poets write about what they can't help writing about*. When I was first teaching poetry, I wrote, "When I sit down to write, it's not a matter of choosing a topic. I write about something because it feels necessary and urgent to write about it. It's more accurate to say that poems choose me."

Part of being a poet is developing a barometer for possible poems. I'm always running experiences, memories, and ideas through my mind to see if I feel strongly enough to write about them, to see if I can visualize a poem's beginning. I also jot down images and feelings in a notebook, as possible seedlings of poems.

In October I drove to upstate New York to give a workshop; the leaves along the Taconic Parkway were fiery red, orange, and fluorescent yellow in the sun. Memories ran through my mind of raking leaves in my backyard as a child, seeing smoke lift from the chimney, feeling crunched-up leaves all over my clothes and face. When I arrived at the school and got out of the car, that unforgettable smell of leaves made my childhood rush back to me. My poetry barometer was rising.

Back in the city, I drove to Brooklyn to visit a friend in the hospital who had just had a baby. In the nursery behind a glass partition were the newborns, all lined up in their beds. Most were sleeping. It seemed so strange to me, all those babies behind glass, all our faces peering in. I thought, is there a poem there? Possibly. I just need to try to write it and find out.

A third possibility came that night as I drove back to Manhattan; at a stoplight, a man in rags walked up to the car and held out his hand, asking for money. Each day in New York I'm asked this question over and over. Emily Dickinson says you know you're onto a poem when "it is like the tooth that nibbles at the soul"; I felt nibbling that night, and a poem started to grow.

• *It's crucial not to censor, especially at the beginning*. Most of my poems travel through many changes before becoming themselves. I always give myself the freedom to fail and put down whatever I want to say, no matter how embarrassing it seems. One of the biggest misconceptions about poetry is the notion that poems come out perfectly on the first try. Except on rare occasions, this isn't true. In order to write well, most poets have to write badly first; to stave off the censoring voice within is an ongoing struggle for poets of any age.

As you begin, here are some things to keep in mind:

• *Prepare the soil*. (See Chapter 1.)

• *Let students decide what they want to write about*. Whether their poems are about stars, being a superhero, a grandmother's death, or the sun, students choose to write about particular things because they care about them. I would have missed so much if I'd decided to have each student write about being a snowflake or a leaf. The only way a poet learns how to discover her own subject is by trying again and again.

• *Create an open, trusting environment*. When students are willing to write about what's really on their minds, their poetry is extraordinary. As a teacher I'm aware that every time I choose to listen instead of control, every time I encourage, and every honest self-revelation I'm brave enough to make bring the classroom closer to being the kind of environment where good poetry can flourish.

• *Spend enough time*. Poets sometimes spend weeks, months, even years writing one poem. It takes a lifetime to be a poet. One day, or even two, devoted to poetry is not enough to give students a deep understanding of what it is.

• *You don't have to be the expert*. I can't tell you how many teachers have come to me and said, "But you're a poet. I would never feel comfortable doing this. I don't know enough about poetry." Learning something new can be difficult; at first the rewards might not seem worth the upheavals.

Be willing to learn alongside your students; tell them you're going to be learning about poetry together. You can even write with them and read your poetry attempts aloud as they do. Teach each other.

Recently I was cleaning out the closets in my apartment and came across an almost-new briefcase tucked away among hats, sweaters, and scarves. I bought it to use when I first started teaching poetry; I can't imagine carrying it now. My time in the schools has taught me, sometimes gently and sometimes not, that my own authenticity as a teacher is more important than any costume or pose. I've always eventually come back to writing and saying what's important to me, wearing what I'm comfortable wearing. As you start to teach and learn about poetry, you don't need to carry a shiny briefcase. And your students don't have to bury poems in time capsules. Together you need to listen as carefully as you can and trust the integrity of your own voices when it's time to speak.

3

"Someone Who Will Truly Listen": Conferring

When I arrived at Stanley Kunitz's house I felt embarrassed clutching the bouquet of pale flowers. I had heard about his magnificent garden but had never imagined anything as spectacular as this: rows and rows of magenta, purple, and yellow flowers I didn't know the names of, Japanese bonsai trees, blossoming vines, sweet smells wafting through the yard. I wanted to throw my meager bouquet in the bushes, but I was afraid that he might see; I held it tightly as I opened the gate to enter his yard.

After I rang the bell Stanley emerged from the shadows of the room. As he got closer I remembered again how he looked; he still had that wise face.

Every year since I was a student and Stanley my teacher, I visit him for a reading of my poems and a little poetic inspiration. This annual conference feeds me throughout the year. That day, on my first visit to his summer house, I handed him my bouquet with apologies; he graciously admired it and found a vase. We sat in carved wooden chairs by a bay window that over-looked the sea. It was low tide, and I could see wide bands of tan, blue, and green, and the white shapes of anchored boats.

After catching up on the year's news, I handed him three poems. He took them and began to read. I watched his eyes move back and forth, as I listened to my own quick breathing; the paper crinkled in his hands. Near me was a basket of beautiful stones; I pulled it nearer and picked one up for good luck.

After a few minutes he looked up. "You've gone through a revolution," he said. I put the stone aside. "This poem is rooted in the flesh and blood of your experience. It's not an artifact, like some of the poems from your student days."

I got out my notebook to write everything down, feeling the nervousness and excitement some of my students must feel. He went on. "What you used to write were poems removed from your experience and your feelings," he said. "Now they're all one."

He noticed! By some miracle he saw reflected in my work the changes my life had undergone. We also talked about changing a word or breaking a line in a different place, but what stayed with me was the truth he spoke, not just about poetry but about my life: his recognition of my struggles to change.

Near the end of the visit, I asked him for any last advice. He said, "You must first create the kind of person who will write the kind of poems you want to write. You're on the right track. I'm still working on it, at eighty-two." He had that sparkle in his eyes.

The light outside turned deep blue. It was time to go. He walked me through his garden to the gate; we said goodbye and hugged, and I left. Already the new poems I would write were swimming in my head.

As I walked down the street I felt elated—it was actually possible to live the life of a poet; Stanley had testified to this. Once again he had given me what I keep going back for. He had helped me with some insights into my poems but, more important, he had given me a sense of hope, of belonging, of reassurance that I was headed in the right direction, that what I've been trying to be and to write is all part of what a poet does.

As a teacher, I try to remember what Stanley has done for me and to offer it in turn to my students. What can I say that will make a difference? What has encouraged me is not questions about this line or this word or vague, generalized praise, it's the big things Stanley has noticed, the sense of being listened to and understood. This is the crucial element in responding to any-one's poetry.

My education from colleagues at the Writing Project also has been invaluable. From Lucy Calkins I learned, among many other things, the power of listening. In her book *The Art of Teaching Writing* she says, "It is listening that creates a magnetic force between writer and listener. The force of listening will draw words out; writers will find themselves saying things they didn't know they knew."

This kind of listening isn't passive; it involves giving someone the feeling of being known and understood, as Stanley does for me. In traditional writing classrooms—the classrooms I grew up in—the topic was assigned, the writing accomplished, and the product handed in for evaluation. There was seldom any listening or indeed any interaction at all among teacher, student, and writing. When I began to teach poetry, I used the only model I knew: the one I'd learned as a student. But after five years of working with Lucy Calkins and Shelley Harwayne and other colleagues at the Project and of reading about other process approaches to writing, I started to respond to students' poems very differently. I became a listener; as Lucy says, I started to teach the writer of the poems, not the poems themselves. I stopped trying to fix each one and thought more about the larger issues I could teach each student, according to where he was as a writer.

William Stafford writes about conferring in his article "The Minuet: Sidling Around Student Poems": "I am the follower in this dance. . . . I must hover about the poems rather than plunging into them. . . . Surely the direction is to be toward the writer's own taking over of the writing." The difficult task for me as a teacher is to confer with my students honestly, without writing the poems for them or becoming the leader in the dance.

A few years ago a colleague and I embarked on a research project on the teaching of poetry. I learned many things that year, but maybe the most important had to do with responding to students' poems. When I was a researcher, each poem was valuable to me, no matter how small or unsuccessful, because it told the story of what that student felt and knew about poetry, offering invaluable insights into the student's life. But only if I looked and listened hard enough, trying to withhold my evaluations and judgments, could I gather an entire history of each poet. From what they said about their poems I started to understand so much more about them as writers; what had been a one-sided conversation between their poems and my evaluations and directions became an opportunity to explore the richness of what was behind the words.

In the course of my research I also learned to see patterns in many early drafts of students' poems and therefore could suggest some of those strategies to other students. As a teacher of teachers I worked with teachers and students in the classroom differently from the way many poets work. My job was to teach teachers how best to teach poetry; we worked with students side by side. This is the context in which these classroom scenes took place.

It is afternoon in a classroom in Queens. Most students are hunched over papers, writing; some are looking at the wall or out the window. As I walk around with Mrs. Johnson, I try first to gather an overall sense of what everyone's writing about. Some have chosen the rain, some their families, one a dog, one stars. I like the variety in the room. They've chosen different topics according to what's important to them that day; it will make the poetry and the class more rich and give us more to explore together.

There's so much I want to tell them: how poems don't just happen, how poets often write several drafts before they know what they really want to say. Mrs. Johnson notices that most have begun with titles: "My Dog," "Rain," "Love." We make a note to remind them not to let titles box them into a subject, that writing poetry is a process of discovering what you want to say. I have to remind myself that just as writing poetry is a process, so is teaching poetry. What I want to give teachers and students is a deeper appreciation and understanding of poetry; there are many days ahead.

Before I confer with anyone, I like to get an overall sense of who's writing what, who's stuck, who needs what kind of help. If I notice that some people haven't found anything to write about, I let them think for a while. It's difficult to write a poem on command; I can't count the number of times I've sat in thought waiting for an idea to come. If some still can't think of anything after a few minutes, I might talk with them individually or gather them into a group and discuss some of the beginning strategies mentioned in the previous chapter.

As I look around the room I spot Jason. He has written three lines, and his pencil is down. We walk up and crouch beside him.

"Hi, Jason. How're you doing?"

"I think I'm finished," he says, looking at me and smiling.

"You're finished!" I hope I don't sound too surprised. "Will you read your poem to us?"

He looks so eager and pleased with himself.

> Cats are cute.
> Cats are great.
> Cats can't be beat.

The old me wants to evaluate Jason's poem. The researcher, the curious me, notices what Jason knows about poetry. There's some rhythm in his poem, repetition, and a little rhyme; it sounds like a chant or a cheer. He definitely knows the difference between a poem and a story. I tell him what

I notice about his poem, but I also want to know why he chose cats as his subject.

"Jason, I'm wondering," I say, "what made you decide to write about cats today?"

"Because I have a cat," he says. He's beginning to lead me into the dance, and I need to make sure I follow.

"You have a cat?"

"Yep."

"So this poem is about *your* cat, then?"

He looks down at his poem. "Well, sort of. It's mainly just about cats."

"What were you thinking today when you decided to write about cats? What made you write this today?"

"Well," he says, "when you were talking about getting a picture in your mind, I closed my eyes and saw my cat. So I decided to write my poem about him."

"You just closed your eyes, and all of a sudden it came to you what to write about?"

"Yep."

"Will you close your eyes again, and tell me what you see in your mind, what you saw before when you saw your cat?"

His eyes close tight, and he speaks slowly. "Well, I see my cat. He's curled up on my bed. I love him. I pretend that he's my son." He quickly opens his eyes.

" 'I pretend that he's my son,' " I say back to him. "You know, what you just said sounds like poetry. You really helped me *see* your cat. I wrote down what you said; let me read it back to you." After, I continue.

"A lot of poets do what you just did: first they put their ideas down, then they go back and think again and see if there's anything else to say. Closing your eyes seemed to help you really see your cat. You don't have to stop there; you could keep thinking, and you might want to write down more things that come to your mind. That's how a lot of poets write their poems. You might want to try it. I'll be back."

When I return later, Jason has finished again, this time for good.

My Cat

My cat is black and white.
I pretend that he is my son.
I love him.
His feet smell like popcorn.

I'm delighted, and surprised at how different the two poems are. I read them both back to him and ask what he thinks. He likes the second better; when I ask why, he says he can feel his cat in it more.

"The next time you write a poem," I say, "you can do that same thing. Just write your ideas down, then go back and try to picture more, and add that to your poem."

There are two main thoughts I like to keep in mind when I'm conferring with students about their poems. First, I want to find out what guided the writer in writing the poem. What made Jason write about cats or Michelle write about stars? Why that today? I often think of the beginning poem as the tip of an iceberg, just the top portion of its hugeness showing. My job is to find out what's underneath—which is the second thought I keep in mind. What does the rest of the iceberg look like? What's underneath, what's not yet written?

One strategy that helps in uncovering the iceberg is "re-visioning." "Revision" means literally seeing again; that's what Jason did in the second poem about his cat. Instead of listing more small facts—his cat's name, when he got him, his color—he "re-visioned" the experience, pictured it and then reexperienced it. He used the image as a resource, something to build on; then he was able to reconnect with what sparked the poem into existence and generate more ideas from there. If he had decided not to write his new thoughts about his cat, that would have been fine, too. For the next poem he wrote, he still would have learned the strategy of closing his eyes and using the image.

Poets' first drafts are often place-markers. James Merrill says, "The words that come first are anybody's . . . then you have to make them your own." Jason's first words about his cat were anybody's; his later poem sounded only like his own. When he spoke his words sounded more like poetry than what he had first written. This is quite common—it's as if, in the writing, students translate their idiosyncratic ideas into "Poetry," and everything changes. Part of my job in the beginning is to help them discover that what they say, or what they see in their minds, is often the kernel of a poem. They don't have to translate their words into some fancy, "poetic" language.

Over Donald's shoulder I see he has written about Transformers, the popular robot toys. I'm curious about this poem, about Donald, about what's going on for him and why he chose to write about this. I need to find out what Donald thinks.

"Donald, what's up?"

He stares at his paper, avoiding my gaze. "Fine," he says. "I'm finished."

"What do you think?" I'm really curious about his reaction to his poem.

He shrugs. I try to follow his lead

"Donald, I noticed you just shrugged your shoulders." He smiles a little. "What does that mean?"

He responds in a soft voice. "It's okay."

"What are you thinking?"

He looks at me for the first time. "Well, it's kind of boring."

I repeat what he has said, trying to understand. "You think your poem is boring? How come?"

He shrugs again.

"Let me ask you something," I say. "I'm curious. What made you write about Transformers today?"

With a little more life, he says, "I don't know. I just couldn't think of what else to write about, so I wrote about Transformers."

"Sounds like you're not too happy about it."

He slowly shakes his head.

"Do you want to keep working on this poem?" He pauses for a long time. Then he shakes his head no. "That happens to me sometimes," I tell him. "I start a poem and then after working on it a while I realize I don't really˙ want to write it. And that's okay."

He looks relieved, as if I've given him a welcome way out.

"Is there anything else you'd rather write about?" I ask. "Anything that's been on your mind lately?" Mrs. Johnson's look at me signals yes.

Donald pauses for a long time, as if deciding whether or not to trust me. "Yeah, my baby sister," he says finally. "She's sick. She's in the hospital. She has this disease." A long pause. "I miss her a lot."

I put my arm around him. From Transformers to this! How many times have I done the same thing, written about who knows what in order to escape the thing that really matters most?

"Is this something you might want to write about?" I ask.

He looks at me. "Yeah."

"Lots of people think that poets sit down, have an idea, write a poem, then put it in a book," I say. "I wish it did happen that way. But it hardly ever does. Sometimes it takes me a while to find out what I really want to say."

One of the most important things I've learned from my own writing is that just because you start a poem doesn't mean you've discovered what you want to write about. If it *is* what you want to write about, the poem probably won't emerge looking anything like its beginnings. Richard Hugo, in "Writing Off the Subject" (*The Triggering Town: Lectures and Essays on Poetry and Writing,* 1979) says about writing poetry:

> A poem can be said to have two subjects, the initiating or triggering subject, which starts the poem or "causes" the poem to be written, and the real or generated subject, which the poem comes to say or mean, and which is generated or discovered in the poem during the writing.
>
> Young poets find it difficult to free themselves from the initiating subject. The poet puts down the title: "Autumn Rain." He finds two or three good lines about Autumn Rain. Then things start to break down. He cannot find anything more to say about Autumn Rain so he starts making up things, he strains, he goes abstract, he starts telling us the meaning of what he has already said. The mistake he is making, of course, is that he feels obligated to go on talking about Autumn Rain, because that, he feels, is the subject. Well, it isn't the subject. You don't know what the subject is, and the moment you run out of things to say about Autumn Rain start talking about something else.

Part of my job in conferring is to find out if the writer is interested in what he or she has written; if not, I have to show him or her the door, the freedom not to have to keep writing something boring. On the other hand, students often *do* want to write about Transformers or other things I might consider unimportant, but I must try to keep this bias to myself and find out why the idea is important to the writer. There is nothing inherently wrong with writing about Transformers; I simply need to discover the bond between the subject—whatever it is—and the writer. Why Transformers today? What is the spark?

Nikki's poem reads like this: "I took a trip to New York City. We had a lot of fun. The moon was big and pink up in the sky. All the stores were open late." I crouch beside her, say hello, and ask how it's going.

"Fine," she says. "I think I'm finished."

"You're finished. So what do you think?"

"It's okay," she says. This seems to be a standard response in this class.

"One thing that really helps when I finish a poem," I say , "is to have someone read it to me. I listen to see if I can get any more images in my mind, to see if I've left anything out or if something doesn't sound right, or to see if it's really finished. Can I read yours to you?" I read the poem slowly, with respect. I wait out the silence until she responds.

Hesitating, she says, "Well, it kind of sounds like a story."

"The *whole* poem sounds like a story, or just parts of it?"

She stares out the window, looking as though she's thinking very hard. "Well," she says, "it's kind of like a story on the verge of becoming a poem."

I'm impressed that she's picked this up, that she was able to hear it in her poem and articulate it so well.

"Are there places that feel more like a poem and places where it feels more like a story?"

She reads silently, then says, "This part." She points to the lines about the moon. "This part is more like a poem, and the rest is more like a story."

She really is leading me in the dance. "Do you have any idea why this part sounds more like a poem?"

She shakes her head.

"Well, let's look at it together," I say. "Maybe we can figure it out. Let me read this part to you again." After I do, she looks surprised. Rather than telling me, she asks, "Because I can see it?"

"That's interesting," I say, again impressed. "Now you could try and see if anything else comes to your mind. If there's anything else that you can *see*, you might want to add it to your poem.

"Poets start this way a lot; when you just put your ideas down it can come out like a story-poem, like this. The next step is to do what you just did: read it over and pick out the parts that are more poemlike or more interesting and then write from there. The main thing is, even when you think you're finished, to go back and read it again. Listen to it, ask if it's what you want . . . then listen to your answer."

Yolanda has been wandering around the room for some time, chatting with different friends. I wave her back to her seat. She has written this on her paper:

Cats. I think cats are pretty

I dream you dream
We all dream
of ice cream.

"How's it going, Yolanda?"

"All right," she says, a little defensively.

"Are you finished, or are you still working on your poem?"

"I guess I'm finished."

"Which poem do you want to talk about?"

She points to the one about dreams. Years ago I then might have asked, "What else did you dream?" "What are your dreams like?" responding to the content of the poem. Now I try to understand what's going on for her.

I tell Yolanda that the poem sounds familiar, that when I was a girl I knew a poem that went "I scream, you scream." "Were you thinking of that poem now?" I ask.

"Yes," she says.

"It's fine if you want to use the beat of another poem," I tell her, "or let another poem trigger yours, and then change it. A lot of poets do that. But I want to know what *you* think and feel, what's on *your* mind, what *you've* seen or wondered about." I wait. "What about the first poem you started here? What made you start writing about that?"

"I don't know," Yolanda says.

Sometimes conferences are difficult. I feel frustrated and don't know where to go. I try to give the lead back to her.

"Where do you want to go from here?" I ask.

"I don't know what to write about." Yolanda looks disgusted with me.

I ask Mrs. Johnson about Yolanda's experience with poetry. She says it's limited but that Yolanda doesn't write much during story time, either.

"Maybe she needs to read a little more poetry," I say. I had already suggested that Mrs. Johnson always have some favorite poetry books on the shelf, to give to students during writing time.

I go back to Yolanda's desk. "There are some poetry books over there," I tell her. "Sometimes before I write, when I can't think of anything or I'm not feeling too excited about poetry, I go to my bookshelf and read. Usually reading makes me excited and sometimes gives me ideas. Why don't you take a little time to read, and if something hits you and you get an idea, just start to write?"

At the same table is Nelson, who seems to have a problem similar to Yolanda's:

Roses are red
Violets are blue
Sugar is sweet
and so are you

Before when I saw a poem like that I didn't know what to say. But the more I teach poetry, the more I see at least one person in each class write this kind of poem, and I've started to understand why. Poetry is often scary for a beginner; relying on "Roses are red" is a sure path to some kind of success. Many students copy other poems from memory or from books and call them their own. I know this from experience; I did it, when I first started writing: I copied some poems from *Seventeen* and showed them to my friends, saying I'd written them.

Now my response frequently is, "You know, I think I've heard that poem before. Have you heard that poem before?"

Most often they nod.

"I think it's fine if you want to take a poem from memory," I say, "or from a book, one you really love, and write it down. But some other poet wrote it, so it's important that you put down the poet's name or call it anonymous if you don't know who wrote it, to give the poet credit."

I suggest to Mrs. Johnson that it's a good idea for students to have individual notebooks or for her to keep a class notebook into which they can copy poems they remember and love.

"Nelson," I say, "is there anything that's been on your mind lately—something you've felt a lot about, a memory you've had—that you could write a poem about?"

There's a long silence. "Well, I've been thinking about summer," he says, "and last summer, when I went to the beach."

"What do you think? Would you want to write about that?"

Nelson hesitates, then says, "Yeah. But I don't know how to start."

"Poets start writing their poems in different ways. . . . Try this. Close your eyes, imagine last summer when you went to the beach, and tell me what you see."

Nelson scrunches his eyes closed. "I see the waves on the beach. People are swimming . . . "

"Sometimes poets start there," I tell him, "with just exactly the first thing you see. Later you can go back and change things, but that might be a place to start. Remember, keep looking inside your mind for images."

Many times students have an idea but don't know how to begin—especially if they feel a little nervous about whether or not they really know how to write a poem. Sometimes I get them talking about their ideas, then stop them and say, "Why don't you start there? Just write that down." Beginning is the hard part, then things get easier. Sometimes.

A couple of kids at a table are writing poems that rhyme. One goes like this:

> Bats, bats, and a bat
> When he sat, he went splat.

I ask Mrs. Johnson if she'd like to try conferring on this one. She shakes her head. "No," she says with a smile. "I want to see how you handle this." I stoop next to Michelle.

"How's it going, Michelle?"

"Fine."

"Where are you now on your poem?"

"I think I'm finished."

"Hmmm," I say. "Something that really helps me when I think I'm finished is to have someone read it to me, so I can hear how it sounds—to see if it really feels finished. Can I read this back to you?"

She nods. I read the poem. She looks like she's thinking as I read.

"What are you thinking, Michelle?" I ask.

"I like it," she says.

"Great. Any other thoughts about it?"

She shakes her head.

I have to respect what she feels about her poem. But I need to know more.

"Can you tell me what you liked about it?"

"I liked the rhymes."

"Yeah, you do have a lot of rhyming words. How about the way it sounded? Does it feel finished?"

"Yeah."

"I've been noticing two kinds of poems as I walk around. One kind is like yours—short, funny, silly, and rhymes a lot—and the others are poems that have feelings in them. Both kinds of poems are good to try."

I pause. No response. "Where are you going next, Michelle?"

"I might add a little more to it," she says.

"Okay." I turn to Mrs. Johnson to process the conference. "You might even do a lesson on those two types of poems," I tell her. Sometimes when I'm conferring I just gather ideas that I can tell the whole class in a lesson, if it's something a lot of people should hear about. "We're trying to focus on the ones with feelings. There's nothing wrong with playing with the language, but when the rhyme is the point of the poem, it's limiting." I also suggest that kids who write rhyming poems exclusively might be given a little challenge: to write a poem that doesn't rhyme, even taking on the same subject, if it's an important one, and trying to write a nonrhyming poem about it.

In the beginning I simply put the conference into the writer's hands. Some questions I ask are:

- How's it going?
- How can I help?
- What do you think about your poem? What are some of your thoughts?
- Where are you now with your poem?

Sometimes I just tell them what I notice about their poems, without asking anything or being evaluative or judgmental.

- I noticed that your first and last lines are the same.
- I noticed you picked something very important to write about.
- I noticed you decided to rhyme here.

I try to keep in mind the questions I mentioned earlier: What made you choose to write about this today? Why was it on your mind? What are your feelings about it?

Sometimes I think I can tell there is more to come, portions of the poem still waiting to be written. I have students close their eyes and re-vision the experience in their minds, then get them talking about what they see, as I did with Jason. That re-visioning is crucial in helping them make the transition from "anybody's words" to their own. Images are a resource that student writers should keep drawing from to make sure what they write reflects the richness of what they see in their minds.

I often read students' poems back to them, so they can hear their own words. I suggest they might want to keep a pencil nearby, to mark places they'd like to work on or things that strike them as powerful. Sometimes they close their eyes as I read, to see if any other images come to mind. Here are some questions I ask:

- What do you think about the poem?
- What were you thinking as I read to you?
- Does it feel complete?
- How did it sound? Any places where it sounded great? Any places where it clanked?
- Did you get any more ideas? Did more images pop into your mind?
- Do you have a favorite part?
- Which part did you feel was most like what you felt?
- Is everything you want to say here?
- Do you like the ending? Do you like the way it begins?

Often students pick up on something they find problematic. Sometimes they discover they don't like the ending, or the poem sounds like a story, or there's a section that doesn't sound quite right. I participate by following their lead, then guiding them toward the next step. For example:

- What could you do to make this part sound better (or more like a poem)?
- What about it doesn't sound right?
- Why does this part sound so great?

In some conferences I refer the student to a specific poet or have her read through published poems to find out how other poets have solved similar problems. If someone is having trouble with an ending, I might direct him to a prepared sheet of poems, a published anthology, or his own anthology to investigate good endings. I tell them all that some of my greatest teachers have been books. If someone has used repetition, I might simply acknowledge it out loud, or I might say, "You did what a lot of poets have done: used repeating words. Here, I'll show you; you did exactly what Langston Hughes did in this poem 'April Rain Song.' " I usually carry a sheet of selected poems to which I can refer as I talk.

Sometimes students are completely critical of their poems, sometimes indiscriminately praising. With the first group I try to be supportive as specifically as I can, while I try to encourage the second group to be more selective in their appreciation. If I help both groups be more specific in their evaluations, eventually they may be able to do this for themselves. I say, "The next time you're writing, why don't you have a friend read it to you? Or read it into a tape recorder and play it back?"

Donald closes his eyes when I read, as if to shut everything out so the images in his mind can have a clear path. Michelle's eyebrows knit as I read to her; a smile crosses her face. Students often tell me their poems sound much better when I read them; they can't hear the power of their own words when they read silently at their desks. Hearing their poems in a different voice helps them get perspective, often more positive.

In addition to these basic strategies, I might talk about more intangible issues—like the role of feelings in poetry. I often asked students how their poems make them feel, and I'd receive a small, quick answer—"Good" or "Fine." But then what?

One question I ask instead is, "Does the poem make your heart beat faster, or not?" Not all poems have to have this effect, but we should feel more than just, "So what?" The Japanese say that after hearing a poem we should feel the "ahness" of poetry; we should feel *something* . Sometimes I suggest that students measure what they have in their hearts against what's down on the paper; if the two are far apart, there's still work to do. Sometimes they find the "So what?" parts and try to rewrite them with more feeling.

It's also important to applaud courage and risk taking. If a beginning poet is brave enough to say what isn't expected or what even may be actively forbidden, I must applaud that courage, no matter how sketchy or prosaic the poem itself may be. Risks may be taken in many areas—language, style, rhythm, or subject—all open the atmosphere of a class.

Revision

Many teachers have approached me unhappily, saying that their classrooms are fine except for one thing: students aren't revising. Revision is a sophisticated skill that takes time to learn; the point of a conference isn't necessarily to have students revise. Often, especially in the beginning, students won't revise one poem; instead, they'll acquire the tools of revision and apply them to each new poem they write. Even many accomplished poets find revision demanding.

In a workshop I once took with June Jordan, she said that the despair you get as you read a poem you've written is not a curse but a gift. It means that you have a vision of how you want the poem to be, and you know it's not there yet. In order to revise, you must get distance on the poem, almost as if it belonged to someone else. Here are a few suggestions I make to students to help them do this:

- Have someone read you the poem or read it into a tape recorder and play it back. Sometimes another voice helps put the poem in a different perspective.
- Put it away for a while. When you take it out again, does it feel new and unfamiliar? If so, it's usually easier to see what's good and what needs to change.
- Try memorizing your poem, then reciting it. Places that are unclear, or that you can't remember, usually need attention.
- Make a drawing of your poem. Are there any gaps in the image?
- Change the point of view. Try speaking the poem to whomever it's about; if it's in the third person, try it in the first.
- Put an equals sign next to each line and free-write to see if more thoughts emerge.

- Write the best line on a new sheet of paper and try the poem fresh from there.
- If there's a word that feels tired or clichéd, write it in the margin and think about it; brainstorm more original words. A thesaurus might be useful here.
- Ask yourself, is this a poem or a story? Which parts are more poemlike, and which more prosaic?
- Tell it to a friend. Sometimes if you imagine saying your poem to someone you care about, the language becomes more natural and more urgent.

Once I get distance from my work, I need to know what to do about the problems I've identified. Sometimes I need a broad, encompassing strategy and sometimes only minor editorial techniques. Here are some of both:

- *Delete unnecessary words*. Language that's commonplace or redundant drains the poem of energy; if it's not fresh and vital, take it out.
- *If necessary, delete whole sections*. Sometimes a poem requires radical cutting; the first part may be just a warm-up for the second, or the ending may repeat what's already been said. Don't be afraid to delete a lot.
- *Experiment with line breaks*. Does energy leak out of any of the lines? How do they look on the page? Break the lines in different ways to see what works best; don't settle for how they happen to fall on the page the first time.
- *Reorganize*. Is there another line that could begin the poem? Is the ending buried somewhere in the middle? Sometimes rearranging can make a surprising change.
- *Strengthen your verbs*. Verbs are the engines of sentences; if yours are dead, the poem will stop. Whenever possible, choose the active over the passive voice ("the wind blew the leaves" versus "the leaves were blown by the wind"); this lets the poem move with less hindrance.
- *Consider the title*. People often skip titles when they read poems aloud; is yours connected and crucial to the poem, or does it feel stuck on? Usually I save the title for the end and then choose among several, instead of using the first that comes to mind.
- *Leave gracefully*. Maxine Kumin says that poems are like lovers; you can forgive almost anything if the ending is good. Does the poem feel complete? Does the ending satisfy you? If not, is there a more satisfying ending hidden elsewhere in the poem?
- *Consider punctuation*. Try your poem with punctuation and without; do you notice a difference? If you've decided to punctuate traditionally,

do the periods and commas make your poem move the way you want it to? If not, you might want to experiment further.

Revision isn't easy and sometimes isn't necessary; many students write wonderful poems without revising at all. Learning to revise well takes years; for us as teachers, the purpose of a conference is to learn and to offer options to the writer, at whatever stage of the process he may be.

Evaluation conferences

Once the workshop is under way and I start to have a sense of who my students are, my conferences change. I begin to know their strengths and weaknesses, and our talks are informed and altered by that understanding. Conferring piece by piece starts to feel fragmented; instead I like to have what Nancie Atwell has called evaluation conferences.

Following Nancie's example, I ask students to spread out all the poems they've written and try to evaluate them, to get a feeling for who they are as writers. Some questions I offer as guidance are:

- What things do you usually write about?
- Any obsessions?
- What kinds of poems do you tend to write? Rhyming poems, long, short, narrative, lyric?
- What kinds of lines do you usually work with? Long or short?
- What are you really good at? Titles, images, interesting words, repetition, rhyme?
- What are you not so good at? How would you like to improve?
- Do you revise? How do you do it? Do you change or add a word or overhaul the whole poem?
- What's the hardest part of writing a poem for you? Where do you get stuck?
- Are there any new things about poetry you'd like to learn?

It's important that students first try to evaluate themselves, then for us to go through this process with them.

One student—Courtney, in sixth grade—read through her poems before our conference. She decided she used language and images well; her main concern was that the poems were so abstract that sometimes people didn't understand them. Her titles reflected this: "The Rain Falling Inside Me,"

"Illusion." She was able to pinpoint her strengths as well as her weaknesses. I suggested she study poets who write concretely, like Cynthia Rylant in *Waiting to Waltz* (1984), a book of poems about everyday experiences written in ordinary language. I also told her about Langston Hughes and described the way he writes about very abstract things but always uses vivid images, which make the poem accessible and alive.

After that, my conferences with Courtney changed. I knew her more deeply as a writer; I knew what she was trying to do, what her goal was for herself. This gave our talks new focus and purpose.

Sometimes students want to know how to write rhyming poems, or how to make poems longer, or write with deeper feeling, or revise. These conferences give us information beyond what we learn from poem-by-poem appraisals. Both are important: the slow, word-by-word practice and the stepping back to see the whole.

There is no one way to have a conference. The strategies discussed here are certainly not the only ones I use; I also talk about line breaks, language, and much more. (Later chapters deal with these topics separately.)

As the brown bat in Randall Jarrell's *The Bat Poet* (1963) says to himself, "The trouble isn't finding someone who will hear the poems. The trouble is finding someone who will truly listen." Curiosity. Listening. Trying not to write the poems for my students according to my vision. Letting them discover their own way. This is what responding to students' poems is all about. It's the biggest challenge we have as teachers.

4

Sound and Silence: Line Breaks and White Space

Recently I heard Gwendolyn Brooks read her poems at Barnard College. Someone requested that she read her famous poem, "We Real Cool." I was curious to hear how she would read it. I had been using her poem in workshops to demonstrate skillful line breaks, to show how after each line of a poem the reader pauses, even if only slightly.

Time after time teachers have said to me, "But I was told in college to read right through the line break, as if the end of the line didn't exist." I was told this, too. But I know that I write my poems in lines; when I read, I pause at each line break. Professors probably tell us not to pause to prevent us from exaggerating the pause and treating it like a period.

Hearing Gwendolyn Brooks read her great poem would settle the controversy once and for all. She started to read:

We Real Cool

The Pool Players.
Seven at the Golden Shovel.

We real cool. We
Left school. We

Lurk late. We
Strike straight. We

> Sing sin. We
> Thin gin. We
>
> Jazz June. We
> Die soon.

There was a long pause after the second "We." By putting the second "We" on the same line as "We real cool," Brooks created a rhythm that sounded like jazz. This strategy also emphasized the "We," the characters in the poem. My doubts were assuaged.

Robert Frost said, "Writing free verse is like playing tennis with the net down." In this chapter the net is the lines of the poem and the spaces surrounding the lines.

Line breaks

On the first day of one workshop in Brooklyn, Molly, a second grader, comes up to me, hands me her poem, and says, "I'm done." My first glance at the page tells me that her poem is written in one large block, like a paragraph of prose; it doesn't look like a poem. I follow Molly back to her desk.

"After a poet finishes her poem," I tell her, "the next job is to put it into poetry form." I take out a sheet of some of my favorite poems and show them to her.

"See how poetry has different shapes?" I say. "It looks different from a story. Poems are like buildings; some are long and skinny, sometimes with only one word on a line. Some are fatter, with much longer lines.

"Now you have to decide how you want your poems to look and sound. In your poem, after every single line, my voice is going to stop a little— because in poetry, blank space means silence. Let me read you your poem the way you have it written, and you tell me what you think."

She crinkles her nose as though she doesn't like it. "It sounds too choppy," she says.

"So what you need to do is read through your poem; wherever you hear your voice pause, put in a slash mark to mark the end of the line. Let's do the first couple of lines together."

"Every day an old woman would sit on a bench / and feed pigeons . . . " Molly marks the end of each line with a pencil. (See Figure 4–1.)

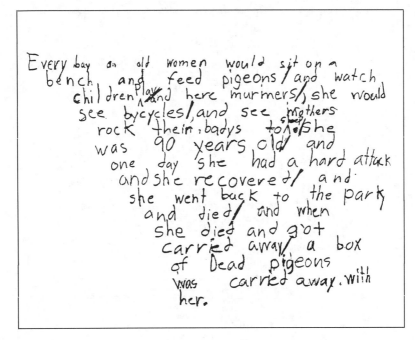

Every day an old women would sit on a
bench, and feed pigeons / and watch
children play and here murmers / she would
see bycycles / and see mothers
rock their badys to she
was 90 years old and
one day she had a hard attack
and she recovered / and
she went back to the park
and died / and when
she died and got
carried away / a box
of Dead pigeons
was carried away. with
her.

Figure 4–1   Molly's piece

"I'm going to go and see what other people are doing; you keep going. When you finish putting in the slash marks, write it out on another piece of paper and see if you like the way it looks. If a line is too long, or if you don't like the way it breaks, try it a different way. Experiment with it."

I come back later to see what Molly has written. (See Figure 4–2.) She has broken the poem into lines that are nearly sentences, but she has experimented with line breaks, her first attempt to impose structure on a poem.

After I read Molly's poem, there's a line of children behind me, all exclaiming, "I'm done, I'm done!" Instead of having an individual conference with each of them, I decide to teach about line breaks in the next day's lesson, using Molly's poem as an example.

The students are gathered around me on the floor. "Yesterday," I start, "a lot of you came up to me saying, 'I'm done, I'm done!' When poets make a poem, one thing they have to think about before they can say it's done is how they want the poem to look and how they want it to be read. Yesterday I worked with Molly on putting her poem into poetry form."

Figure 4-2   Molly's poem in lines

I had written both drafts of Molly's poem on a big chart. Molly reads them both aloud and explains why she broke the lines where she did. That would be enough, but another example has value, too. On a large chart I had written two versions of William Carlos Williams's "Poem." "I also want to show you another poem," I say, "where breaking the lines makes a big difference. I'm going to read both of these versions out loud, and maybe you can tell me what differences you hear."

Poem

As the cat
climbed over
the top of

the jamcloset
first the right
forefoot

carefully
then the hind
stepped down

into the pit of
the empty
flowerpot

Poem

As the cat climbed over the top of
the jamcloset first the right forefoot
carefully then the hind stepped down
into the pit of the empty flowerpot

As I read the first version, I accent the white spaces between the stanzas. The words are like the cat's movement, creeping around the room and into the flowerpot. The second version sounds more like prose; if a cat's movements were like the rhythms of this poem, it would probably fall headfirst off the jamcloset.

But the first is uncomfortable and awkward sounding to my students, who are used to the smooth sounds of poetry read like prose. I ask them all to close their eyes and imagine the cat making its journey quietly, slowly over these objects. Have they ever watched a cat moving over delicate objects? What's it like?

They show me with their hands and bodies the slow, stealthy movements of the cat.

So how should the rhythm be?

"Slow," they say.

"Let me read the two poems again," I say. "Which sounds more like the rhythm of a cat?"

I hope many of them now understand the care a poet takes with line breaks.

One of the most basic units of organization of a poem, and one that affects not only how the poem looks on the page but how it sounds, is the line break. It is as fundamental to a poem as a sentence or a paragraph is to a story— maybe even more so. No poem can be called finished (unless it's a prose poem) until the author has organized the poem into lines.

In the beginning, students finish poems very fast; I usually find myself talking about line breaks and the poem's shape on the second or third day. Getting them to think about deliberate line breaks keeps them from abandoning their poems too soon; it asks them to go back and consider what they've written. For many students, revision begins here. They go back and reread their poems, listening for the pauses but also to every word, to the poem's sound. As they read, they begin to listen to their own voices, which may tell them that a word doesn't sound quite right or that the end or a particular line doesn't work. Listening for the line is a crucial first step in building a deeper understanding of a poem.

Here are some line-break fundamentals I try to teach over the course of the workshop:

- Every line is broken in a particular place on purpose, so the reader will pause there.
- The way lines are broken affects the rhythm of the poem. Longer lines usually make the rhythm more proselike; with shorter lines, the poem will be choppier, breathier.
- Each line in a poem is a unit of meaning. This statement should be taken loosely; it doesn't mean you must have only phrases or complete thoughts on a line. Even the word "of" can be a unit of meaning, within the context of the poem.
- Each line should have energy in it; too many small words in one line let energy leak out.
- Line breaks are a personal decision for the poet. There is no right or wrong. There is only what's best for the poem as a whole.

Poets work with both the aural and visual aspects of the poem. A poem's sounds might seem to call for long *and* short lines but look too disorderly on the page. So poets make some changes according to how poems look.

In a television special I once saw on flowers, the narrator said that to us the stripes, lines, and dots on a flower are simply beautiful, something to add extra loveliness to the flower. But to bees they are a code; a little like runway lights at an airport, they guide the bees to the pollen inside. Line breaks serve the same function for a poem; they are a code telling how the poet wants the poem read, an integral part of its meaning and sound.

I suggested to Molly that she read her poem aloud, listening to her natural pauses, to let the rhythm of the poem and her breathing tell her where to break the lines. This is what Coleridge meant when he spoke of "organic form"; the poem's form comes from within, from the rhythms of the language itself.

When I conferred with Dixie about her poem, "Frosty Curtain," I asked why she decided to make some lines long and some lines very short, with just one word. (See Figure 4–3.)

"Because I wanted the words to feel cold," she said, "so I put them on a separate line with nothing else around them—no other words to keep them warm. They're icy by themselves, all alone. It gives you the feel of cold." Her poem integrated the poem's subject with its form.

Many poets work with the tension created by line breaks to change the pattern of the rhythm or to slow the poem down to make people think or to create suspense. After a while, poets often compose the poem in the lines they plan to use. They feel the poem's rhythm as they write it; they don't need to have a prose version first. I tell my students this, that they can try listening to the rhythm of the poem as they're writing it.

White space

During one of my first years teaching poetry, I spent time in Rose Napoli's sixth-grade class in Brooklyn. There, I gave a lesson on blank space, not only the blank space at the end of the line, but that between stanzas, in the middle of the poem. Traditionally this is called the stanza break; in discussing it in the classroom, I called it white or blank space.

In painting there's a common term, "negative space," that describes the shape the air or space makes around, for example, a chair. In a painting that space is just as important as the legs and arms of the chair itself.

White space is like negative space. How the words are grouped on the page is important. It's a serious decision for a poet whether to group lines one at a time, or in twos or threes; it's essential to decide where the blank space should go. It's an issue of sound and silence.

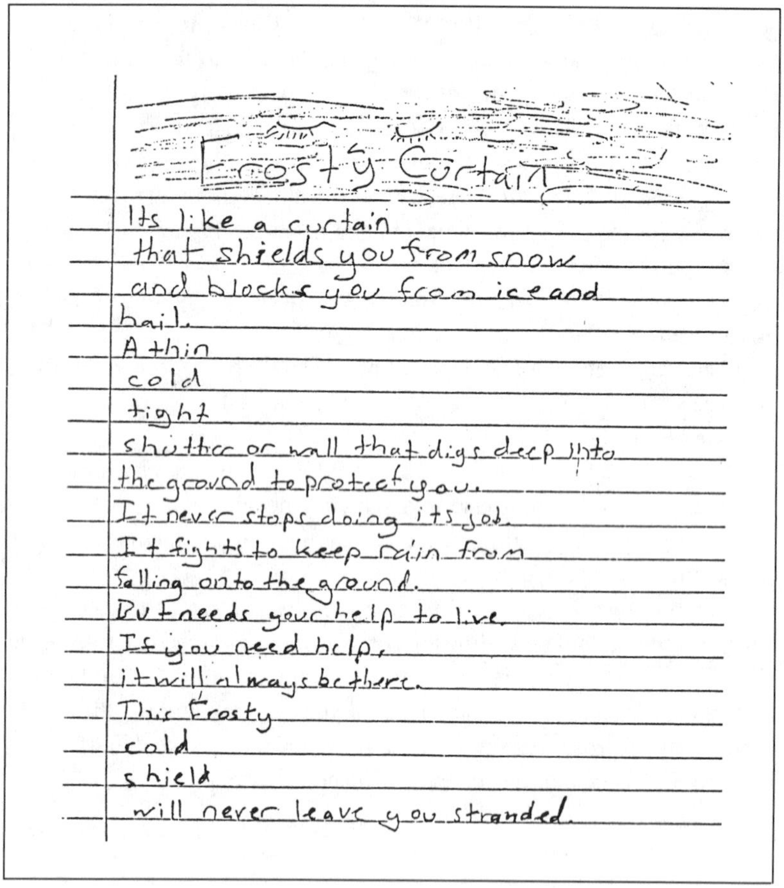

Frosty Curtain

Its like a curtain
that shields you from snow
and blocks you from ice and
hail.
A thin
cold
tight
shutter or wall that digs deep into
the ground to protect you.
It never stops doing its job.
It fights to keep rain from
falling onto the ground.
Bu t needs your help to live.
If you need help,
it will always be there.
This frosty
cold
shield
will never leave you stranded.

Figure 4–3   Dixie's poem, "Frosty Curtain"

Marat grappled with this complex issue when he wrote seven versions of his poem just to get the white space right. When I asked him how he decided to put the poem into couplets, he spread all his drafts out on his desk. First, he explained, he tried his poem with all the words bunched together, but he didn't like the way it looked or sounded. Then he tried it with three lines to a stanza, then four and five, then two; and he liked it the last way best. (See Figure 4–4.) "It just looked and sounded better," he said. Marat trusted his instincts and was willing to experiment with the form of the poem.

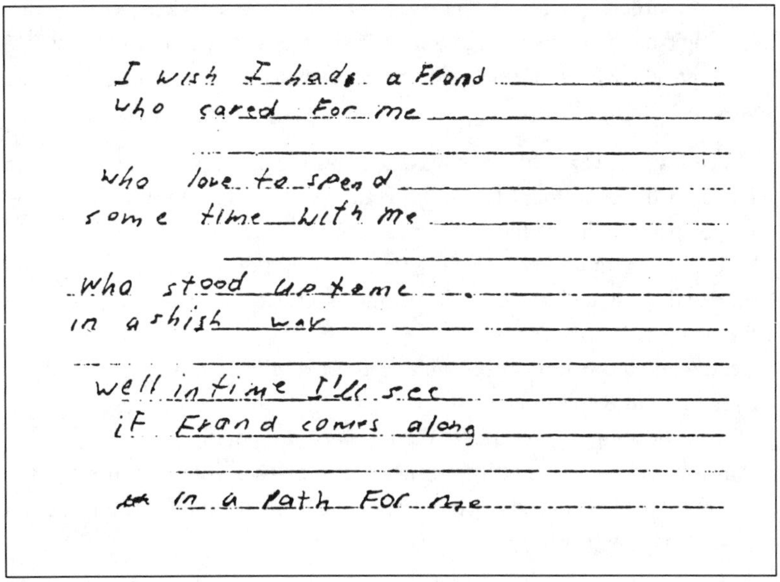
I wish I had a Frand
who cared For me

who love to spend
some time with me

who stood up to me
in a shish way

well in time I'll see
if Frand comes along

in a path For me

Figure 4–4 Marat's poem

It's important not only to focus on the silence in the poem but on the purpose of the stanzas—how many lines you want together and why.

When I was attending Stanley Kunitz's workshop at Columbia, I brought in a poem written in solid lines—there were no stanza breaks at all. After I read the poem, he said, "Why don't you try it in quatrains?" When I asked why, he said he just had a feeling about it, that when he looked at the poem, it felt like the lines were more or less grouped in fours.

I went home and worked on the poem and tried it in quatrains. He was right; with a few alterations, the lines were already grouped that way. I just hadn't seen it.

I tell my students to look at their poems and ask, how do the lines feel? Does it feel like they should be grouped in quatrains, or tercets, or couplets? Some poets set up this limitation before they even start to write. A friend of mine composes in couplets; the limit of the form helps her make the poem.

The concept of white space is similar to that of line breaks. Any time you see space in a poem, it means silence. Poets may use white space to make a break in the information or thought of a stanza; to slow the poem down; to encourage the reader to stop and reflect after a thought; to make the poem look more orderly; to set off the poem's final line and give it more impact; or to single out a line by surrounding it in silence. In the course of the workshop I introduce each of these uses of white space, one at a time. Here are some possible minilessons:

- Type up a poem two different ways to show the difference the white space makes. Choose a poem that uses white space well; then type it with no white space. What is the difference?
- Ask a student to write her or his poem on a chart or on the blackboard and then to discuss with the class her or his process of decision making about the white space.
- Read aloud a poem that uses white space two different ways; what effect does the white space have?
- Discuss how the space affects the mood of the poem.
- Play a recording of a poet reading her poems and ask your students to listen for where the line and stanza breaks fall. Then hand out the written version of the poem and listen to the reading again.

In a conference, I might ask, "Have you thought about the white space in your poem? Do you want any breaks in it? Why don't you read it aloud and listen for any big breaks in the thought; are there any long pauses? Do you like the way it looks on the page? Does it feel like there are too many words clumped together?" Frequently I ask, "What made you decide to break the lines there? What made you decide to put them in threes?" I try to gather information and to be as aware as I can of their process, their thinking on the subject.

Other questions I ask are:

- Do you like the way it sounds read aloud?
- What's the mood of the poem? What's its rhythm?
- Do your lines and spacing help the rhythm?
- Has the energy leaked out of a line?
- Is this the way you want your poem read?

A crucial part of what makes a poem is the tension between sound and silence. When poets write, they concentrate not only on the words, the voices on the page, but on the silence between the words. When both of these forces, silence and sound, are working well together, the poem works, too.

5

Language: The Poet's Paint

With any art form there are givens: a painter has paint, a musician the voice or instrument. And a poet, of course, has words. I've always been amazed that with only the twenty-six letters in the alphabet beautiful words are made, poems are written, and entire libraries are filled. Hallmark cards and Shakespeare both use the same alphabet; as a beginning poet I wondered what made Shakespeare's poems so great: how could those particular combinations of letters have such power?

Poets have to pay attention to how poems sound; we need the poem to please our ear. Yet beautiful music and rhythm alone do not necessarily make a poem. We also need to speak the truth. We hope to express significant meaning and feeling through our words; we want our poems to make people think. But a poem with feelings and ideas and no music is not a poem either. We must have both. Fortunately, they often go hand in hand.

As I'm writing a poem I focus on the words and music as well as on what I'm trying to say. Often these processes are inseparable, and sometimes they happen simultaneously. Yet frequently the bad poetry I read expresses feelings and thoughts with no music in the words, no attention to the language of the poem, so the meaning never gets across.

How do poets pay attention to language? How can we help our students to pay more attention to the music in a poem? I will try to answer these—and other—questions here.

Midway through a poetry workshop in a third-grade Brooklyn class, a student shares his poem with me:

> Snowmen are nice
> Snowmen are fun
> I like snowmen.

Much of the students' work sounds like this: poems that don't evoke any specific image or feeling, whose music is flat and uninteresting, whose life hasn't yet been found. This can happen when a poet hasn't found something crucial to write about, but even the students whose topics were carefully chosen have written poems that seem to rest inert on the ground, unable to leap into the air as poetry. It is as if their wings are broken, and they have no means to fly.

I decide to gather my students together to discuss this with all of them. "For me, poems are often the result of looking at something I've seen over and over again, then trying to describe it in a new way," I tell them. "Then when you read the poem, it leaps off the page; it takes your breath away. It surprises you.

"Let's try it together," I say. "If we were going to write a boring, ordinary poem about an apple, how might it go?"

"It's red," someone shouts.

"It's good to eat."

"I like apples."

"Boring!" the kids yell, as I write our attempt on a chart.

"I have a poem about an apple where I think the poet saw the apple in a new way; she really *looked* at it. The poem surprised me at the end. I'm going to read it."

Apple

At the center, a dark star
wrapped in white.
When you bite, listen
for the crunch of boots on snow,
snow that has ripened. Over it
stretches the red, starry sky.

NAN FRY

I read the poem twice. Many kids close their eyes as I read. After the second reading there are smiles and oohs and aahs.

"Let's try another one," I say. "If you were going to write an ordinary, boring poem about clouds, how might it go?"

"They're white."

"They're fluffy."

"They're in the sky."

"Now listen to this poem about clouds. Is this any better?"

> The dark gray clouds,
> the great gray clouds,
> the black rolling clouds are elephants
> going down to the sea for water.
> They draw up the water in their trunks.
> They march back again across the sky.
> They spray the earth again with the water,
> and men say it is raining.
>
> NATALIA M. BELTING

Again there are smiles of surprise and delight. This is how we should feel when we finish reading a poem. We should feel refreshed.

The kids go back to their desks to write. I'm curious to see if this idea will make any difference to their poems that day. Many of their poems seem transformed. (See, for example, first-grader Stacey's poem in Figure 5–1.)

Instead of beginning with the definitions for simile and metaphor—"a comparison using 'like' or 'as'"—I begin with the reason why poets use these techniques: to transform the banal into the poetic. To surprise the reader. To describe something in all its complexity. For example, Amy's poem begins, "I feel like an army/the smoke and cannon/in the sky." Other examples are shown in Figures 5–2 and 5–3. As the poet Yehuda Amichai said in an interview:

I think metaphor is reaching out. We are groping for words. We say, "Ah, I'm looking for words. I can't express myself." So we need something, again something *real*. Because if I want to say, "He's such a cruel man," I might say, "His heart is stone," which is also an over-used expression, but you are *groping* for words. You want to keep your head above water, so words become a kind of, I would say, *solid* thing, which you can hold to in order to make yourself understood. I personally believe that the invention, so to speak, of the metaphor is the greatest human invention, greater than the wheel or the computer. (*American Poetry Review,* November/December 1987)

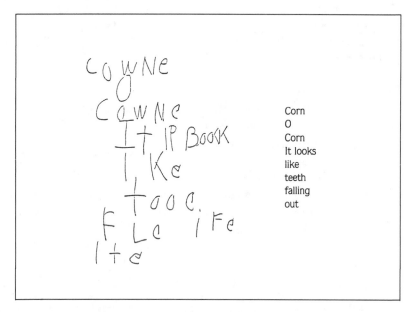

CO WNE	Corn
O	O
C QWNC	Corn
It IP Book	It looks
I, Kc	like
Too C.	teeth
F Lc iFc	falling
Ite	out

Figure 5–1   Stacey's poem

Figure 5–2   Roger's poem

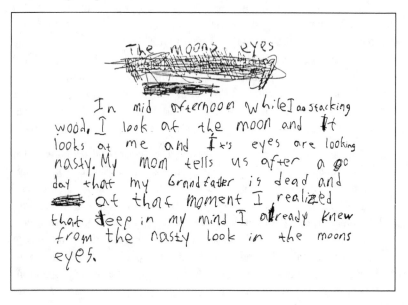

Figure 5–3   Candice's poem

I don't think it's wrong to tell students about simile, metaphor, and personification, but the explanations should have an organic origin. These tools should come when you need them, when you're groping for words; they shouldn't be forced on you because you're supposed to use "like" or "as" in a poem. Taught out of context, without an understanding of how poets use them, the labels become another way to turn students off of poetry—to make them yawn at the mention of the word.

Jennifer, a third grader, had written a poem; what made it so extraordinary was this line: "The glory colors in the sky." "Glory colors"—what a remarkable combination of words! Jennifer hadn't written "red and blue colors" or "brilliant colors"; instead she used a word that sang and surprised and simultaneously was so true to her description.

A few days later, when I went back to the class and conferred with Jennifer, I noticed that she had changed the word "glory" to "glorious"—a more conventional, less original description. When I asked what had made her change it, she said, " 'Glory colors' doesn't really make sense. It's not really a word." I knew something was up. I asked where she had heard this, and she confessed. When her teacher had read her poem a day earlier, she'd told Jennifer that "glory colors" didn't make sense and that the proper word was "glorious." So Jennifer had changed it.

When I asked Jennifer what she meant when she used the word "glory," she got very excited. She said, "The colors are smooth and deep in the sky"; she seemed to see them again as she spoke. When I asked the same question about "glorious," she didn't know what to say. I suggested that sometimes poets use an odd word or combination of words and that sometimes just that word can make poetry.

I called the teacher over and explained this to her and then showed Jennifer the first line of "April Rain Song" (see p. 26).

" 'Let the rain kiss you . . . ' " I read. "He didn't say, 'let the rain fall on you,' he said, 'Let the rain kiss you.' Just like you said 'glory colors.' Doesn't it make the poem more poetic? Doesn't it make the whole line different?"

Poets work long and hard choosing the right words for a poem—original words that evoke a vivid image, words whose sounds are right. In a mini-lesson I sometimes teach, I eliminate one or two words from a poem and ask students to come up with replacements. Sometimes I use an excerpt from Robert Lowell's "Mr. Edwards and the Spider" (the words I eliminated are in brackets):

> I saw the spiders [swimming] through the air,
> [marching] from tree to tree that [mildewed] day . . .

In one class in Amherst when I asked for suggestions to replace the first word, the students shouted, "Spinning!" "Weaving!" When I asked for something a little more unusual, they yelled, "Dancing!" "Rolling!"

Lowell chose each word for the image it evoked; he turned down "hot day" in favor of "mildewed day," which brings back the smell of mildew in a basement: wet, humid, hot dirt. He also considered the sound of the words—which sounds better, "a hot day" or "a mildewed day"? The second set of words is richer in our mouths, more pleasurable to say.

With older students I introduce the use of the thesaurus. I suggest they read through their poems and underline words that feel tired and clichéd and then make a list in the margin of other words that might work better, using the thesaurus to help.

I also suggest that students look for and replace overused words—words that appear over and over in their poems. As an example, I might tell them about a poem I wrote called "Alexandria." A sentence in the first draft read, "I spit the dark seeds / out on the highway." "Dark" is one of the words I tend to overuse; it is a catchword for a variety of emotions. I knew I needed to change it, so one day I looked through the thesaurus and came across the word "gloomy"—which sounded more interesting and more accurate.

In another minilesson, I ask the class to list a few words that have gone stale, like nice, pretty, fun, great, beautiful. Sometimes you can use these words in an original way, but often they're just crutches that don't really say what we mean. In one class I asked a boy's permission to use his wonderful poem about the sea to illustrate this point. He had said in one line, "It was so beautiful." I went around the room asking the students to close their eyes and say what they found beautiful about the sea. Of the ten or so people I asked, each had a different answer. Some said the sea was "blue and foamy and the waves," while others talked about the sand. The boy needed to write what he saw.

The trouble with very general words is that they don't give us a vision. Specificity, strong images, vividness, and concrete words all help to make poetry poetry, to get it off the ground. May Swenson says, "A poem is not only *about* a thing; it *is* a thing, a construct unlike any other made of language."

Poetry is different from prose in that you don't only use the words to communicate the sense; the words are an end in themselves. When I write I attach myself to the language, to the fact that a word has real power in the world. Most kids lose that power in schools because they hear many poems using shopworn words, or they hear poems where the content is funny but the language isn't, or poems with just a message, without beautiful language.

I once saw my colleague Suzanne Gardinier teach a minilesson about this.

"What I want to talk to you about today is words," she said. "Probably the most important part of a poet's body is her or his mouth; that's where I try out words, to see if they might be good to use in a poem. Today I was looking around and saw this word on a sign: chrysanthemum. Chrysanthemum. Try saying it, see how it feels in your mouth." The room was filled with the sound of the kids trying to wrap their mouths around the word.

"I carry a notebook," she told them, "where I write down words I love; sometimes I don't know what they mean, I just like the sound of them. Sometimes they're words I know. I write them down; then when I write my poems, I usually have some good words floating around in the margins, at the edges of the draft, that sometimes make it in.

"This is a poem by a Nicaraguan poet named Yolanda Blanco, called 'It's Raining'; the Spanish words in it don't stand for other words, they're names of towns in Nicaragua. It's kind of like a weather report; the words feel so good to hear and say."

It's Raining

It's raining
in Teotecacinte Cusmapa
in Tepesomoto Cuspire Saslaya.
Big puddles
covered the roads of Sinecapa
the Tule Yaoya and Mayales.

If you go to Limay take your raincoat
and it's also raining in the Macuelizo
in Ciminguasca and Alcayan.

Everything is nice and green in Tisey in Totumbla.

It's drizzling in Guisisil
thundering in Yeluca and Apají.
In Nandasmo continual storms.

I've been soaked in all Nicaragua
it's raining now.

YOLANDA BLANCO

"Now take a minute and think of a word you love," she suggested, "that you might want to use in a poem. Try it out in your mouth." Someone said "Zimbabwe," another, "crash," and someone else, "supercalifragilisticex-pialidocious."

She held up a draft to show them. "A second grader wrote this," she said. "It's called, 'Crunch, Crunch.' The first time he wrote it, it went like this:

Crunch, Crunch

The ice is a cruncher.
Crunch, crunch goes the ice.
I love the ice.
My baby sister loves the ice.

"I read it to him and asked him to listen and see how it sounded. When I finished, he said, 'There's something missing, but I don't know what it is yet.' I told him I'd come back later and see if he'd found it. When I went back, the poem read like this:

Crunch, Crunch

The ice is a cruncher.
Crunch crunch goes the ice.
I love the ice.
My baby sister loves the ice.
All the cars go fishtailing.

" 'Fishtailing!' That one word completely changed the poem."

In Rose Napoli's class I asked Marat, a boy from the Soviet Union, to bring in one of his favorite poems in Russian. I gathered the children around him, and Marat read the poem. A flurry of sounds and music went through us. The poem was so beautiful, it sounded like a song we partly understood and partly didn't. We understood the tone of it, the rhythms, but not specifically what it said.

Marat then decided to embark on a translation project. He faced the problems all translators face; as Robert Frost said, "Poetry is what gets lost in translation." When Marat translated the poem literally, much of the poem's music was lost. But if he changed the poem too much, he would lose the poem's meaning.

Translation is a project many bilingual students could try, to begin to focus on language. You could even give an entire bilingual class the same poem to translate, to see and hear the differences.

In many classes I teach a minilesson on using the dictionary. I start by saying how much I love dictionaries, that they're so exciting. Instead of using them for spelling, I read them like a Sears catalogue. I open one and read the students some words. Sometimes a word will just knock at your head—maybe the word "galoshes"—then by some magic it ends up in a poem.

Sometimes I talk about verbs; I tell my students that verbs are the engines that make sentences move. If you don't have an engine in your sentence, it will just sit there. "Let's take this sentence," I might say. " 'I walk down the street.' Does that give you a picture in your mind? How could you give that sentence a good engine?" Some kids would yell out, "I crawled down," "I ran," "I struggled," "I dashed." All those are much more interesting and concrete than just plain "walked."

Sometimes I pretend a word is like a geode: rough and ordinary on the outside, hiding a whole world of sparkling beauty inside. My job as a poet is to crack the words open to find that inner treasure. One of my students visited California and told me there were lizards everywhere you reached. He showed how some kids had gone "like this"—he twirled his hand in the air like a cowboy—and the lizard's tail had broken. "How would you say that in a poem?" I asked. One of the things a poet does is describe the in-describable. "The kid whirled the lizard," he said slowly, "and it fell off its tail." He took the dull way of explaining and transformed it into his own.

In conferences we can guide students to focus more on the language of the poem. I might suggest to students:

• Go through your poem and underline any clichés or tired, overused words. Then find better ones, either by brainstorming them or searching for them in the thesaurus.
• Underline great words you've used.
• Take out any extra words that don't contribute to the energy of the poem.
• Have someone read the poem back to you. Listen for places that feel boring. It might mean the language is uninteresting and needs work.
• Watch out for places where your poem clanks, where the rhythm is off.

Most of us are so concerned with sense that we don't get enough enjoyment from the sounds and pleasure of words, the way they sing. We don't think enough about how they feel in our mouths as we read or how they make our bodies feel. As one poet says: "Quite simply, a poem should fill you up with something and make you swoon, stop in your tracks, change your mind, or make it up, a poem should happen to you like cold water or a kiss."

And it's all done with those same twenty-six letters.

6

Tennis and Racquetball:
On Form

At the Fort River School in Amherst, Massachusetts, toward the end of their month on poetry, I introduced a sixth-grade class to a complicated, fascinating form: the sestina. They'd been writing free verse for weeks, and I thought they might want to try something new. To begin, I had quoted that comment of Robert Frost's that I've already used here to define the importance of form: "Writing free verse is like playing tennis with the net down." After the lesson, one girl walked up to me, a little incensed at this new fly in the ointment of poetry, and argued with Frost's statement. "Well," she said, "playing tennis without a net is just racquetball. And I *love* racquetball." I was speechless. How could I argue with her? And yet, I also understood and sympathized with what Frost meant. Stanley Kunitz had once said the same thing: "The whole concept of form depends on the setting of limits. There has to be a weave and a cross-weave in order to make cloth." But that student was right; why does it have to be tennis? Why can't it be racquetball? This is the dilemma of form versus free verse.

When I first started to write poetry, there was so much I had to learn. I felt threatened by the world of formal poetry, thinking that poets who wrote using traditional forms were the real poets and knew the true secrets of poetry. My consolation was that, yes, they may know the secrets, but they're the secrets of "old-fashioned" poetry; what I was trying to do was new and modern, breaking fresh ground. All this might have been true, but the more

I wrote and studied the more the division between formal and free verse began to shift and fade. Instead of being warring countries, the two are neighboring territories in one great nation.

Formal poets (and their poetry) are somehow unfeeling, some people think. When I was starting out, I imagined their houses to be lifeless, spotless, and cold. On the other side, the "free-versifiers" were groovy; they had rock 'n' roll records and tapestries on their walls. As I look back on this, I'm astonished at how powerfully insecurities act to create artificial polarities, different enemy nations.

I used to argue in the classroom that formal poetry breeds cold, unfeeling poems; free verse encourages genuine expression. The danger here was ignorance, my own ignorance in the truest sense of the word: I didn't fully understand where form fit into the world of poetry. To begin and end a poetry workshop praising and encouraging only the work in the two forms most favored by educators—haiku and cinquain—seems ridiculously limited, just as presenting poetry only as image or as the expression of deep feeling is limited. Both approaches leave poetry in the place it's always occupied: on the periphery, instead of in the foreground as a wonderfully rich, vital art that people have worked at for many, many centuries, sometimes devoting their whole lives to it.

And so what's to be done? The solution lies in understanding exactly what is meant by form in poetry. But that's a book in itself. The formal aspects of poetry are too complicated and abundant for me to handle in this one chapter. There are, however, many reference books to which teachers may turn for guidance. (See p. 165 for a sampling.)

Although I rarely write in traditional forms or use rhyme, I've experimented with the villanelle, the sestina, and various forms of rhyme and learned a lot from this experimentation. It probably helped me put my poems together better. It's worth experimenting with.

Driving in the car in the evening, my mother would sometimes burst out with, "Red sky at morning, sailors take warning. / Red sky at night, sailor's delight." We'd look at the sky, and if it was a beautiful sunset, we'd know the next day we'd have nice weather.

Or sometimes at night I'd search the sky for the first star against the still blue background of twilight; as soon as I had spotted it, I'd try to hold it, with words: "Star light, star bright / First star I've seen tonight . . . " Somehow it made my day seem luckier, more full of hope. Sometimes we'd be out walking, and I'd spot a penny on the sidewalk or grass and would exclaim, "Find a penny / Pick it up / All the day / You'll have good luck." And I believed I would.

When I'm listening to a song I like on the radio, I have a hard time not tapping my foot or nodding my head to the beat. I can feel a great song all over my body. Rhythm is physical; it feels good. And this is one of the magical qualities of rhymed poetry: its rhythms and recurring sounds give us pleasure.

But many of the sayings I remember also hold some truth. It's not just rhythm for rhythm's sake; it's the combination of truthfulness and music that makes some verses memorable. In poetry, it's crucial to have both.

One of the ways rhythm is made is through rhyming. The linking of rhyme sounds in our ear initiates a rhythm that threads the rest of the poem together. One does not have to rhyme in order to make rhythm, but rhyme is the most obvious, most popular aspect of poetry. Easily recognizable, providing music, joy, even surprise, it is one of the oldest ways of constructing a poem, and one that can be beautiful.

There are dangers in rhyme, though, and I think teachers are aware of them. For many students it's still seen as the exclusive definition of poetry. It's also difficult to do well and tends to force students into focusing exclusively on the rhyming words, diverting them from the authentic.

I used to avoid it; I even summarily banned it from the workshop. But eventually I decided to confront it. After all, rhyme has a great tradition in poetry; it's not just Shel Silverstein. Now I have integrated rhyme into the poetry workshop, and students use it as their net, far better than I ever believed they could.

I usually wait until the workshop has solidly begun before I introduce rhyme: by then, students are writing about things they care about and have a basic grasp of fundamental aspects of poetry like line breaks and the image. Because I'm trying to expand my students' sense of what makes a poem a poem I don't introduce rhyme at the beginning, when they usually identify it as *the* single element that defines poetry.

Readers get pleasure from hearing the music of language, the words chiming with one another, but they also ask poems to reveal meaning. It doesn't have to be serious, but it should matter in some way. A lot of poets settle for one or the other; when you read their work, you can hear that something is missing. I can't count the number of times I've been in a classroom and read poems that go something like this: "The cat is fat and flat / He got in the hat and then went splat." It rhymes, and it's musical, but obviously it lacks something. I always tell students that it's important that they try to have both sound and sense in their rhyming poems, as Aisha did in hers. (See Figure 6–1.)

Rhyme should also contain many variations. Sometimes I think of rhymes like faces: a good rhyme shows character and reveals something about identity; a weak rhyme is like an expressionless face, smooth, showing no emotion, no hint of what that person is like. A rhyme like "mean" and "lean" or "cat" and "fat" could perhaps be made interesting, depending on its context, but basically it's barren of possibility. A rhyme like "parade" and "cavalcade" has more texture to it; not only does it show more character, but is sounds better musically. It feels better to say.

Learning to listen for interesting rhymes is an important part of learning to write good rhymed poetry. Take for example this poem, by third-grader Sang:

Young Horse Running

Leaves leaping in the air
He had to rake them everywhere
He had to find the new green clover.
There was a fence for jumping over.

The rhyming words "air" and "everywhere," "clover" and "over" are pleasing to the ear, and the poem, for the most part, isn't forced. A rhymed poem

Figure 6–1   Aisha's poem

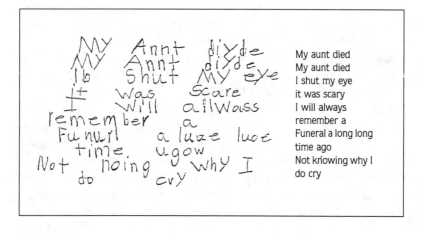

My aunt died
My aunt died
I shut my eye
it was scary
I will always
remember a
Funeral a long long
time ago
Not knowing why I
do cry

is forced when the meaning seems secondary to the rhyme; the whole poem feels like it's desperately trying to rhyme, not to say something true using rhyme as a tool. In this poem, the message is conveyed using rhyme, and it all makes sense. (See also Figure 6–2.)

The most common way students rhyme poems is to rhyme a one-syllable word with another one-syllable word. This can get musically tedious; it offers few surprises and little variation. The poem may get too sealed and sterile. A reader may suspect that the sole reason the poet uses a word is to suit the rhyme scheme and that he obviously didn't spend enough time trying to find something better. The reader then loses faith in the writer. It's important for the reader to feel that the poet is in control and is writing with both the sound and the sense of the poem in mind.

The human ear loves to hear a surprise in a predictable rhythm or meaning. As teachers we play a role beyond that of reader; we can guide our students by exposing them to poems that rhyme well and by reading back our students' work and listening for solid rhyme.

One way to vary the rhyme is to use multisyllabic words, like "master/disaster," or words that rhyme two syllables such as "pardon/garden." Another method is to use slant rhymes, which are those that are not perfect, like "bread" and "offered."

Figure 6–2 Using rhyme

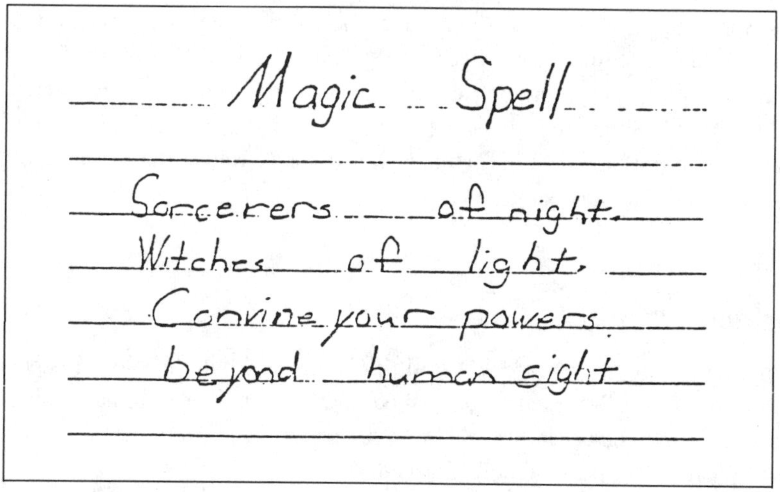

Magic Spell

Sorcerers of night.
Witches of light,
Convine your powers
beyond human sight

Most of the rhymed poetry students write in the beginning uses end rhymes: the last word in each line rhymes. This can be very obvious or can be disguised.

The beauty of the end rhyme is that it organizes the poem. It sets up a rhythm we come to expect. But again, poets must try to avoid using obvious and predictable rhymes that will make the poem boring.

Poets sometimes diminish the monotony of an end rhyme by breaking the line so that its end isn't the end of the sentence. Our eyes are forced to read on to the next line quickly to finish the sentence. This device is called *enjambment*.

Many poets use only internal rhyming or combine it with end rhymes. In internal rhyming the rhyme words are contained in the middle of poem; the effect is that of an echo, rather than drumbeats. Swinburne wrote, "Sister, my sister, O fleet sweet swallow." The rhyme is less obvious, and the poem's rhythm is less emphatic.

I encourage students to experiment with their rhymes. In the beginning, many are so pleased just to get a rhyme at all that they use the first word that comes to mind. It's crucial to revise, to think about what the best rhyming word is for the job. Many poets use rhyming dictionaries, so they can have many possibilities among which to choose.

I also suggest that students think first of what they want to say and write a line, then work the rhymes from there, thinking "How can I best sing this?" This avoids the frustrating experience of thinking of rhyming words as you write and then hitting a dead end where the only word you can find doesn't say what you mean, when you have to backtrack and write all over again.

Sometimes, though, the rhyme dictates the meaning of the poem and allows the writer to create a diversionary stream. In Elias's poem in Figure 6–3, rhyming made Elias look at water in a new way, and his poem explores those new feelings. In Ratanak's poem (Figure 6–4), rhymes like "moon" and "bedroom" feel like soft chimes, yet Ratanak was not even aware of putting them in his poem.

Repetition

In a kindergarten class a boy was sitting at his desk with a colorful paper in front of him. I walked up and asked how he was doing. He had drawn a vivid brown object in the middle of his paper.

"What's your poem about?" I asked.

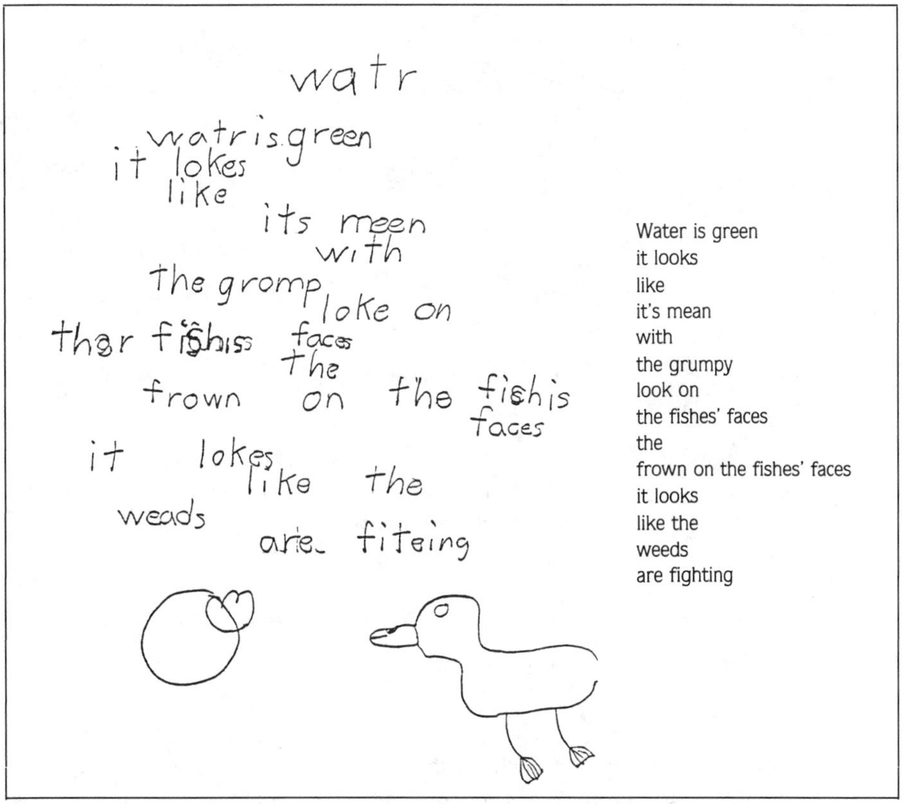
watr
Water is green
it looks
like
it's mean
with
the grumpy
look on
the fishes' faces
the
frown on the fishes' faces
it looks
like the
weeds
are fighting

Figure 6–3 Elias's poem, "Water"

He didn't have a poem, he said. But the picture he'd drawn was about his gerbil.

"You know, it's the craziest thing," he said to me. "I give him a carrot, and he plays with it. I give him a ladder, and he climbs on it. I give him his water bottle, and he chews on it . . . "

When he'd finished, I told him, "You do what a lot of poets do; you keep repeating things." I'd written down what he'd said and read it back to him. "It makes it sound kind of like a song . . . like a poem."

He looked at me with a big smile, surprised and proud that he had made a poem without even knowing it. Then he attempted a few letters.

Most of the time repetition happens naturally, as in Sona's poem. (See Figure 6–5.) I point out the repetition as it happens naturally, but sometimes

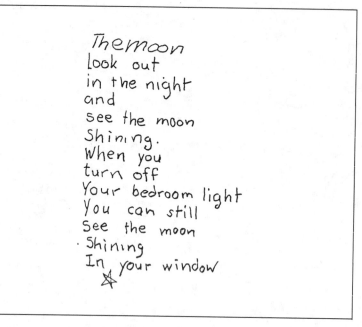

Figure 6–4   Ratanak's poem, "The Moon"

I introduce it in a lesson as something they might want to experiment with. I'm careful not to introduce just one way of using repetition, though; instead I give them a myriad of ways to explore.

I also talk about how natural repetition is. Sometimes when I'm excited about something, I'll say, "Today I saw a big tree. It was the biggest tree I've ever seen. It was so big . . ." Repetition sometimes serves to emphasize a point. Sometimes it glues a poem together, making it sound more musical; as with rhyme, you hear the chiming of words. And sometimes poets set up a predictable repeating pattern, then vary it for surprise.

Refrain

During my first year of teaching, a seventh-grade student named Chrystal wrote a poem about the death of her dog. (See Figure 6–6.) I'd never mentioned repetition. But after she read the poem to the class, we talked about it, and then many students decided to experiment with it.

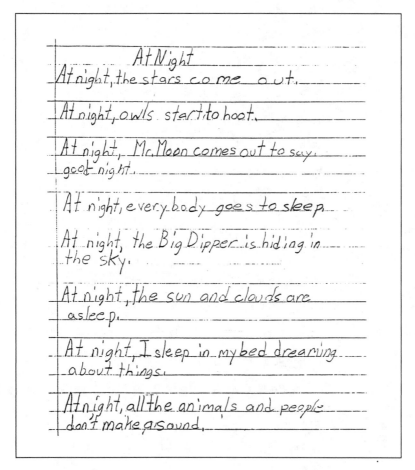

Figure 6–5   Sona's poem, "At Night"

As with all poems, Chrystal's repetition is just a hook on which to hang the coat of the poem. She began with an idea that was important to her, then decided to keep repeating the line, "The fun that little dog brought." Some poets vary the repeating line; but Chrystal decided to vary the narrative, so that the refrain line resonates with meaning. Eloise Greenfield used a refrain in a different way in the poem "Things" (see p. 27); her refrain changes to make the end line of the poem.

Poems using refrains sometimes sound like chants—the oldest, most primitive form of song, like a magic spell to ward off evil spirits. Many songs on the radio use the refrain.

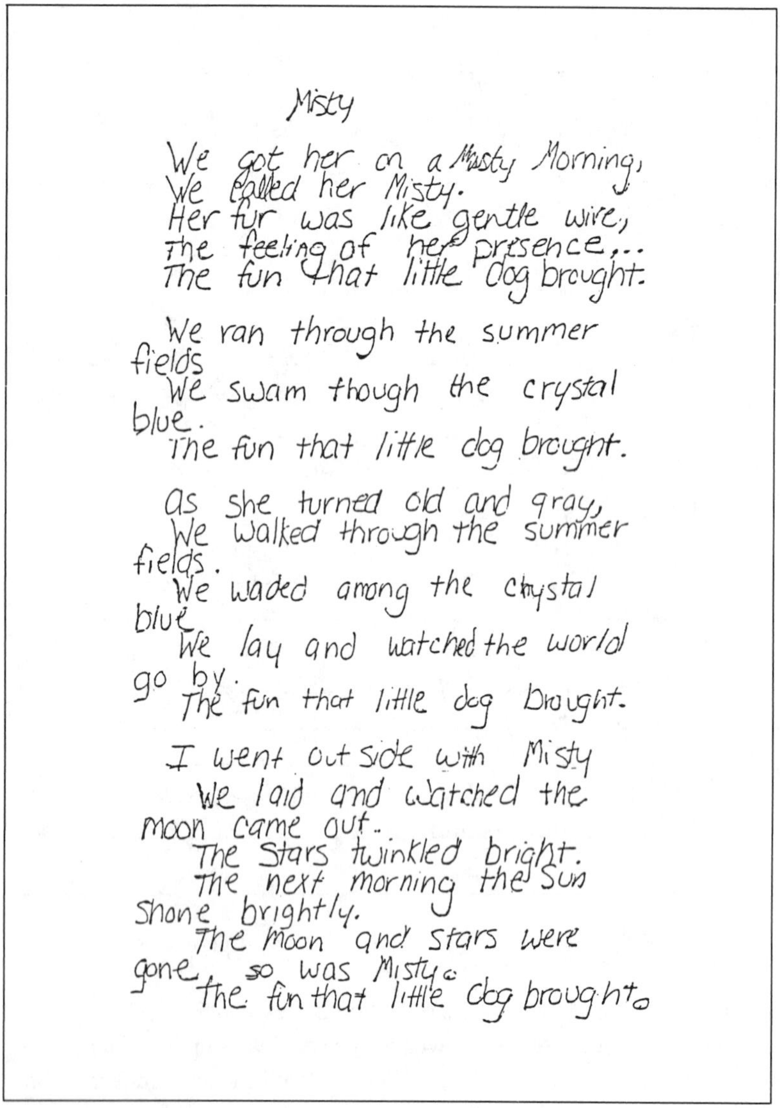

Misty

We got her on a Misty Morning,
We called her Misty.
Her fur was like gentle wire,
The feeling of her presence,...
The fun that little dog brought.

We ran through the summer fields
We swam though the crystal blue.
The fun that little dog brought.

As she turned old and gray,
We walked through the summer fields.
We waded among the crystal blue
We lay and watched the world go by.
The fun that little dog brought.

I went outside with Misty
We laid and watched the
moon came out.
The stars twinkled bright.
The next morning the Sun
shone brightly.
The moon and stars were
gone, so was Misty.
the fun that little dog brought.

Figure 6–6   Chrystal's poem, "Misty"

One thing to remember about repeating lines is that it almost always sets up a rhythm, a music. Take these lines from the top of my head:

I have to wait here.
I have to wait here.
I have to wait here.
I have to wait here.

This isn't by any means poetry, but the repetition sets up a music that could be the kernel of a poem. Students may even want to experiment by putting repeating lines in poems they've already written, to see how it changes the music.

Many poets use repeating lines in their poems without using a refrain. In some poems, the first line is repeated as the last line. The last line gathers the poem up and turns it around on itself.

In William Carlos Williams's "To a Poor Old Woman," he repeats "They taste good to her" three times, varying the line breaks to make the reader see and say the line differently each time.

To a Poor Old Woman

munching a plum on
the street a paper bag
of them in her hand

They taste good to her
They taste good
to her. They taste
good to her

You can see it by
the way she gives herself
to the one half
sucked out in her hand

Comforted
A solace of ripe plums
seeming to fill the air
They taste good to her

In Walt Whitman's great poem, *Leaves of Grass,* he is able to include so much of the world because of the form he's chosen. He presents voluminous details but controls them by repeating the beginning of each line. He can go on and on, stuffing the poem with more and more material, and we can take it in, because it's categorized.

Some people call this kind of poem a list poem, because once the form is set up you can list anything. I suggest this form to students with a lot of information to get across. It's like taking an inventory.

Stanzas

The word "stanza" comes from the Italian, and it means "room." When I open an anthology, I see poems with a variety of different kinds of rooms. In some, the words are written all together, with no spaces between the lines; there's just one room. Others are divided into neat little squares, very orderly and clean.

The variations of stanzas are endless. The three traditional stanzaic forms in English are the couplet (two lines to a stanza), the tercet (three lines), and the quatrain (four). Traditionally these were rhymed, but the terms now refer also to unrhymed lines grouped the same way. Stanzas without any fixed pattern are called "verse paragraphs."

Some poets set up their stanza plan before they write the poem; others write first, then experiment with the form. Whether or not to write in stanzas is a personal decision, as line breaks are; but whatever choices a poet makes will change the visual and aural attributes of the poem. If the poem is good, the visual and aural formats will be in perfect harmony.

As with line breaks, it's important to remember that the space between stanzas isn't neutral; it is an intentional silence. If there's no reason for a reader to pause, the white space will not make sense. As with negative space in painting, the absence is as crucial to the work's integrity as the presence; poets deliberately and carefully work with the tension between silence and speech.

Genres

Many teachers are bothered by how similar many student poems are to stories. If a poem tells a story, they figure, how can it be a poem? On the other hand, among my students at Teachers College, some of their biggest struggles were to write poems that were intimate, that deeply involve their feelings.

What a lot of people don't know is that there are genres of poems. There is a tradition of poets writing both these kinds of poems: the narrative and the lyric. I'll discuss here the lyric, the narrative, the epic, and the dramatic.

Many students are relieved when I tell them they're in good company when they express their feelings in a poem; poets have done this for hundreds of years. They're writing lyric poems, named after the musical instrument, because many poems were once songs accompanied by the lyre. Lyric poems are often personal and emotional; they're usually shorter than narrative or epic poems, and they often sound like songs.

A narrative poem tells a story. What usually distinguishes it from prose is its music; sometimes it uses rhyme, sometimes repetition, sometimes a more loosely organized rhythm. It should feel more compact than a story. The poem "Misty" by Chrystal is an example of this. (See Figure 6–6.)

A long narrative poem is called an epic, from the Greek word *epos*, meaning a speech, story, or song. Whitman's *Leaves of Grass* is considered an epic, as are of course *The Iliad* and *The Odyssey* of Homer. Epics usually try to explain an entire world or present a story.

A boy once came up to me in a school in Brooklyn, looking very frustrated and claiming he couldn't write poems. When I asked him why, he said that he was only good at writing dialogue, and poems never had dialogue in them. I whipped out my *Norton Anthology,* which I just happened to have in my bag, and opened it to Frost's "The Death of the Hired Man." The whole thing was dialogue, like a play but written in verse. The boy was inspired.

There's a great tradition of dramatic poetry, beginning with the Greeks. One type that many contemporary poets use is the "dramatic monologue" or "persona" poem; the poet tries on the mask of another person and speaks through it. Robert Browning, in "My Last Duchess," and T. S. Eliot, in "The Love Song of J. Alfred Prufrock," were masters of this form.

I had the pleasure of having poet and teacher Myra Cohn Livingston visit a classroom in Queens for one day. It was within a few days of beginning a poetry workshop, and I watched her confer with a few students. Using one of her techniques, she asked a student who was writing a poem describing leaves to pretend she *was* a leaf and write from that perspective. The revision was astounding. It helped the poem to become more poetic and helped the poet to get out of her ordinary voice (See Figure 6–7.)

Using persona is a familiar technique for many kids. I remember that the neighborhood kids and I used to play elaborate games in our back yards;

I'm a Leav

I'm a leav dancing in the wind
the wind stops
I stop
I start dancing agian
Swish swosh I go
I pick up a brown leav and dance

Figure 6–7   "I'm a Leaf" by Sari

Figure 6–8   Peter's poem, "Undarkening"

Undarkining
I am the sun,
I lighten updark spots,
gazing down at children yelling, screaming,
old people talk old times,
I lighten up the world,
I am a smbal of joy,
I am the sun

sometimes we pretended we were horses or pioneers, sometimes Native Americans, sometimes nuns under the willow tree with towels on our heads. It's a natural part of play and curiosity. Figures 6–8 and 6–9 are examples of poems by students writing in the voices of objects or other people.

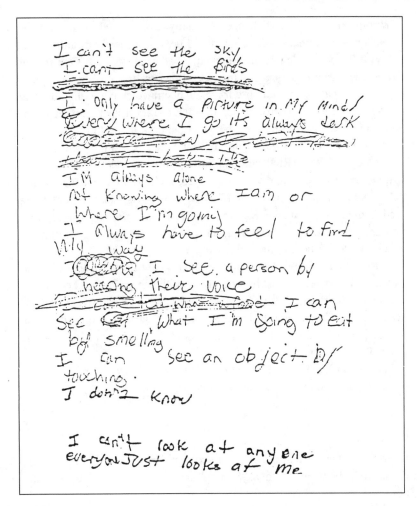

Figure 6–9   Lisa's poem

Form

When poets speak of writing "in form" or of writing "formal poetry," we usually mean arranging the poem in a specific, set pattern that already has been established. Most of these forms were developed centuries ago, like the sonnet. The patterns are still recognizable, but poets have written many variations on them since they first appeared.

Writing in form is a challenge; I usually don't introduce it until the workshop is well under way. Even then I present it mostly as an option.

"Why do poets write like that, anyway?" some students ask. One answer I've learned from experience is that sometimes traffic, grocery shopping, and all the banalities of daily life force the poetic voice into hiding; having a pattern to follow, a puzzle to solve, often coaxes it back into the open. Sometimes we can see an object better in the dark if we don't focus on it but look a little to the side; writing formal poetry is a similar trick.

The poet Adrienne Rich said that writing in form was part of her early writing strategy: " . . . like asbestos gloves, it allowed me to handle materials I couldn't pick up bare-handed." Many other poets acknowledge having used form this way. Stanley Kunitz says, "It helps to train the ear"; having to take such care with the poem's construction develops concentration, which can help a poet in the writing of free verse as well.

Unfortunately, the two forms most teachers know and teach are haiku and cinquain. The haiku at least is certainly a legitimate form, but there are so many other possibilities. It's like serving the same two foods over and over; eventually, students begin to believe that this is what all food tastes like. What about artichokes and herring and falafel? What about the sestina, the villanelle, the ballad?

The forms I'll introduce here are just a few of the many that exist, waiting to be prepared and served in classrooms.

SESTINA

I introduced the sestina to a class of sixth graders in Amherst by reading Elizabeth Bishop's well-known "Sestina" and asking the class to try to figure out its form.

Sestina

September rain falls on the house.
In the failing light, the old grandmother
sits in the kitchen with the child
beside the Little Marvel Stove,
reading the jokes from the almanac,
laughing and talking to hide her tears.

She thinks that her equinoctial tears
and the rain that beats on the roof of the house

were both foretold by the almanac,
but only known to a grandmother.
The iron kettle sings on the stove.
She cuts some bread and says to the child,

It's time for tea now, but the child
is watching the teakettle's small hard tears
dance like mad on the hot black stove,
the way the rain must dance on the house.
Tidying up, the old grandmother
hangs up the clever almanac

on its string. Birdlike, the almanac
hovers half open above the child,
hovers above the old grandmother
and her teacup full of dark brown tears.
She shivers and says she thinks the house
feels chilly, and puts more wood in the stove.

It was to be, says the Marvel Stove.
I know what I know, says the almanac.
With crayons the child draws a rigid house
and a winding pathway. Then the child
puts in a man with buttons like tears
and shows it proudly to the grandmother.

But secretly, while the grandmother
busies herself about the stove,
the little moons fall down like tears
from between the pages of the almanac
into the flower bed the child
has carefully placed in the front of the house.

Time to plant tears, says the almanac.
The grandmother sings to the marvellous stove
and the child draws another inscrutable house.

By the second stanza hands started going up. Some of them identified the
main characteristics of the sestina.

   I explained further that the word *sestina* comes from the Latin word for
"six" and that the poem consists of six stanzas of six lines each, followed

by a three-line stanza to finish. Instead of rhyming words, the poem repeats the same six words at the end of each line in a shifting but consistent pattern. The six words Bishop used are:

1. house
2. grandmother
3. child
4. stove
5. almanac
6. tears

The pattern of the words that end each line is:

Stanza	Pattern
1	1 2 3 4 5 6
2	6 1 5 2 4 3
3	3 6 4 1 2 5
4	5 3 2 6 1 4
5	4 5 1 3 6 2
6	2 4 6 5 3 1
Tercet	5 4 1. Usually, the pattern of the tercet is 5 3 1 or 1 3 5. It is further complicated by the fact that the remaining endwords, 2 4 6, must occur in the course of the lines.

The beauty of this form is its obsessive quality; the poem moves from one place to the next, but you hear the same words again and again—and students don't have to wrestle with rhyme.

Some students thought the form was ridiculous. "Why make poetry any harder than it already is?" they asked. But most of them ended up trying a variation of the sestina and liked what they wrote.

I suggested two ways to begin: they could choose six words and let them lead into the poem; or they could write the first stanza and see what words finished each line. I prefer the second method; that way the poem decides itself, from the inside out. I warned them against using words like "and" and "it" to end their lines, encouraging them to pick significant, concrete words.

Many students asked me if they could write a four-stanza poem or some other variation instead; I agreed. This is where the idea of form as racquetball rather than tennis entered the workshop. It's great for students to move beyond the form to invent their own: a "quatrina," maybe, or a "tercetina."

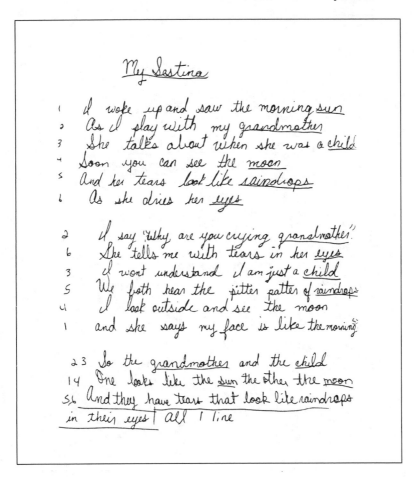

Figure 6–10   "My Sestina"

Figures 6–10 and 6–11 are two examples of sestinas students wrote. Some of the reasons why the sestinas faltered were:

- Sometimes the words were chosen first, without any emotional investment by the poet. The sense was bent backward to fit the form, and the poems ended up feeling and sounding sterile.
- Poets ran into difficulties when they chose boring words, like "nice." Although theoretically any word can work, it's tough to keep a word like "nice" interesting for six stanzas.
- Poets didn't include enough specific words.

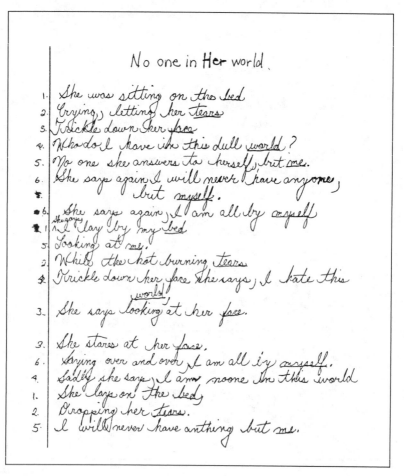

Figure 6–11 "No One in Her World"

VILLANELLE

The villanelle originated in the *villanella,* an Italian folk song accompanied by a dance. The song was passed on until a French poet, Jean Passerat, wrote a villanelle in the sixteenth century that locked the form into its present conventions. A villanelle has six stanzas; the first five are three lines long, and the last is four. Sounds easy enough—but it gets complicated. The first and last lines of the first stanza rhyme and alternately repeat as the last line of each stanza, except the sixth. In the last stanza, the lines are used as the last two lines of the poem. The middle lines of each stanza also rhyme with each other.

The form is more difficult to explain than to see. Here's a villanelle by Passerat:

Villanelle

I have lost my dove:
Is there nothing I can do?
I want to go after my love.

Do you miss the one you love?
Alas! I really do:
I have lost my dove.

If your love you prove
Then my faith is true;
I want to go after my love.

Haven't you cried enough?
I will never be through:
I have lost my dove.

When I can't see her above
Nothing else seems to do:
I want to go after my love.

Death, I've called long enough,
Take what is given you:
I have lost my dove,
I want to go after my love.

Another villanelle to look at is Dylan Thomas's famous "Do Not Go Gentle into That Good Night."

Some suggestions for writing a villanelle:

- Begin with a subject that's important, something crucial; then write the two rhyming lines that will repeat throughout the poem.
- It's easier if the two rhyming lines are big and open; if they're concrete, with specific images, it will be harder to keep hearing them again and again.
- After the two repeating lines are written, play around with the others; it's like working a puzzle. Patience and persistence pay off.

Although I've never had any younger students choose to write this form, my graduate students at Teachers College love it.

BALLAD

The ballad is an ancient form found in most cultures, a story-song used to preserve an important story. Traditionally, it was sung and passed unwritten from one generation to the next. Some of the attributes of a ballad are:

- It tells a story, usually a single event.
- A ballad *shows* us what happened; it's vivid and dramatic, often letting the characters speak.
- A ballad usually represents a public voice, that of a class or race or people, rather than the individual emotions of a single "I" that lyric poetry celebrates.
- It retains many of the characteristics of song: strong story line, plain language, repetition.
- Most ballads are written in quatrains, and only the second and fourth lines rhyme.

Ballads are still used in songwriting: Pete Seeger and Bob Dylan are just two of the many artists who've composed and sung ballads. They're an ideal form through which to tell a story heard in the news, a political event everyone knows about, or a family legend. Although ballads are traditionally written in meter, I suggest to students that they disregard that convention. Ballads may be included in social studies or history; students might want to write one instead of a paper or to use one in a project.

HAIKU AND CINQUAIN

Haiku and cinquain have become the hamburger and hot dog of American poetry classrooms. Ideally, they should be taught as two of many interesting forms, and several misconceptions about them should be cleared up.

Haiku. The dominant feature of the haiku has come to be its 5–7–5 syllable line arrangement; in fact, this is its least important aspect. In fact, ancient Japanese poets counted sounds, not syllables, and seventeen sounds in Japanese are more like twelve to fifteen syllables in English.

The original Japanese haiku tried to link the natural and the human worlds. Contemporary haiku still usually involves nature in some way, although modern poets have written variations on this. Haiku now contain no metaphor, simile, or complete sentences, and most poets writing haiku today create three short, unrhymed lines, the middle slightly longer than the first and last.

A good reference book on haiku is Cor Van Den Heuvel's *The Haiku Anthology* (1986).

Haiku is a wonderful form to introduce in science class, since most haiku depend on careful, detailed observation, an indispensable skill for the scientist. Students might write haiku instead of or in addition to their laboratory or field observations.

Cinquain. The term "cinquain" originally referred to a five-line stanza of any length; early in the twentieth century, Adelaide Crapsey, an American poet, invented the form taught in classrooms today, which consists of five lines of two, four, six, eight, and two syllables each.

There are hundreds of other forms, handed down to the present from long ago and from not so long ago, and many contemporary poets experiment with the invention of form, finding pleasure in stretching and changing the rules, playing racquetball, squash, and Ping-Pong in addition to regular tennis. Writing in any kind of form helps expand a poet's range and trains the ear. It should be an opportunity to play, to experiment with language, and not a test with right and wrong answers. I encourage students to create their own forms, establishing a pattern or a set of rules, and then following it through to see what happens. They can even coin names for the new forms. After all, scientists have the pleasure of naming newly discovered stars; poets can have the pleasure of naming new forms.

7

"The Sun Is Like a Mommy": Kindergarten and First Grade

When one of my younger sisters was of kindergarten age, she went through what I called her "why?" period. On the way to the swimming pool or at home upstairs in my room she would come in and begin the endless questions: Why is there light? Why does the sun go down? Why do the birds sing? Why are you doing that? Why is you hair so curly? Why are you taller than I am? The house was filled with her asking. To some in my family it got to be a little tiresome, but I loved it. I loved her curiosity because it made me think.

One of the most important elements of writing is surprise. Instead of writing "The sun goes down," a kindergartner might write, "The sun gets stuck in the water." At this age their heads are full of wonder and curiosity and questions, and this is reflected in what they say, the startling way they phrase ideas or capture what they feel. A young child sitting at her desk drawing or busily working on something says one word over and over again out loud, or talks to herself, or sings. Language is a new toy, the words fluid in her mouth, the saying a joy. Young children seem to love the taste of language. It's the same love of words that poets have.

One of the first questions kindergarten and first-grade teachers ask me is, "Can my students really write poetry? Some of them can hardly write their names." It's a good question and one I asked, too, before I began teaching students this age poetry. The answer is a definite yes. Some of the best poems I've read have come from these young writers.

99

So how do you do it? How do you get them to go from asking questions to writing poems? There are many ways to begin. As with other grades, it's important to immerse them in poetry first, although kindergarten and first-grade kids often are immersed in poetry naturally. They sing songs together, hear nursery rhymes. So much of how they experience poetry is oral; most very young children "write" their poems by saying them out loud first. I often point out to kids that what they're saying is poetry or that the songs they've been singing are poems with music. I write poems on large pieces of colorful paper and hang them around the room, so they can see how a poem looks on the page, how it is different from a story. They can look up and see and read the poem over and over, to get to know it. Sometimes we make big books of favorite poems, deciding together which lines to put on a page and how to illustrate them. I bring in tapes of poets reading, along with copies of the poems so the kids can follow along.

But be careful of the pitfalls of presenting poetry to young children. Northrop Frye said, in *The Well-Tempered Critic* (1963):

> The infant who gets bounced on somebody's knee to the rhythm of "Ride a cock horse" does not need a footnote telling him that Bambury Cross is twenty miles northeast of Oxford. He does not need the information that "cross" and "horse" make (at least in the pronunciation he is most likely to hear) not a rhyme but an assonance. He does not need the value-judgment that the repetition of "horse" in the first two lines indicates a rather tin ear on the part of the composer. All he needs is to get bounced. If he is, he is beginning to develop a response to poetry in the place where it ought to start.

In one class I was in, the teacher and the children gathered around the piano in the morning to sing some of their favorite songs. They sang for a while, then she asked them to slide over to the rug area. "You know all the songs we've been singing this year?" she said. "Well, these songs are poems, but with music. Today you're going to be trying to write your own poems and songs, using what you know about what's important to you." She gave the kids a chance to think a little bit and then they went back to their desks to write. I could hear some singing, some saying poems out loud; other were drawing pictures or writing a few letters. Some kids were telling stories. The room was rich with sound and song.

In Liz McGrath's kindergarten class at P.S. 176, some kids are sitting cross-legged on the floor. Others are lying on their backs looking up at the ceiling. One is sliding across the floor, having pushed off from the door with his legs as if he were in water. I do my best to get them to sit still, but it's difficult—there's so much energy in them. I know I have to make this short.

"Who knows what a poet is?" I ask. Some of them scratch their heads. A few hands go up. A kid with hair cut close to his head says, "Something that swims in water?" I smile and think to myself, that's one of the best descriptions of what a poet is that I've heard in a long time.

"Well, yes," I say, "kind of." Another hand goes up, and Kahlil asks a question: "Is it kind of a like a pumpkin?"

"A pumpkin?" someone yells.

"No, no!" he yells. Other hands are waving.

"It's someone who writes poems," one boy shouts out, tired of waiting to be called on.

"Okay, does anyone know what a poem is?" I say back.

"Oh, boy," someone says. "Sometimes it rhymes."

"It's kind of like a song."

"A poem is kind of like snow moving." The way some younger kids talk about poetry is like poetry itself.

A few kids begin to lie down and slide on their backs again. I'm reminded once more that I have to make this fast.

"Today you're going to be writing your own poems," I say. "I brought in some poems by poets just your age. I want to read them to you."

I hold up the first one. It's on tan manila paper, stapled together, covered with crayon drawings exploding with color. On one side in pink crayon is the poem, written down the page one word at a time, like stairs.

"Stars, stars are nice. They can float."

The kids' faces are still, amazed. Some shout, "Wow!" I read it a second time, as I often do with poems.

I try to point out a few characteristics of poetry after I read the poem. "See how Stacy wrote this poem, with the words going down like that? She's making it look like a poem.

"Here's another one," I say, "written by Amy. It's called 'Sun.' " (See Figure 7–1.) "When Amy wrote this poem," I tell them, "she was probably sitting at her desk, and the sun was coming in, and she felt it on her arm, all warm. Maybe it kind of felt like her mom hugging her. She could have said, 'The sun is warm—and I like it.' But she surprised us instead. That's another thing poets do: they surprise us, by saying things in a new way.

"Here's one last poem. It rhymes." I read it rhythmically, so they can get the feel of the beat. (See Figure 7–2.)

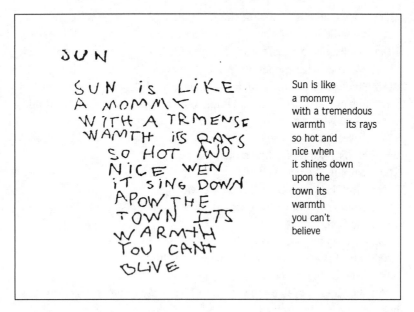

Figure 7–1   Amy's poem, "Sun"

Figure 7–2   Stacey's poem

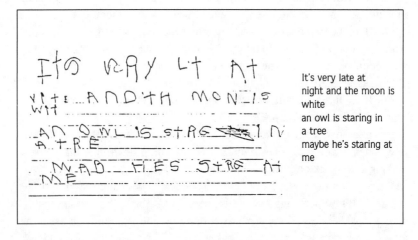

"The most important thing is that all these poems were written about things the poet really cared about.

"So let's just sit for a minute, and you think about what you could write your poems about. You might want to close your eyes and get a picture in your mind—of something you've seen, or something that's been on your mind lately, or a feeling you've had." They are still for a minute. Then I ask them to turn to the person next to them and whisper what they're thinking of writing about today.

It's helpful to show them poems written by kindergarten and first-grade students. One of the biggest fears they have is that they can't write. Seeing the actual writing of other students like them is like an invitation. It's also good for them to see poems both written and drawn so they know they have a choice. This of course should be done in combination with reading them a lot of published poems.

I like to give them a chance to talk to one another about their ideas. (This doesn't mean that they'll stay with their first thoughts; in fact, most kindergarten kids don't know what they're writing about until they draw a picture.) I ask a few to share their ideas; sometimes I do this by saying, "You might already know how your poem's going to begin, and you could say your poem to us."

A lot of hands go up. I call on Robert. He says, "I saw a sun. I already know my poem."

"Will you say it to us?"

He begins, saying each word slowly:

> Sun oh sun
> The sun is not a
> good thing to waste
> sun oh sun rays
> is a good thing to heat
> sun rays is the best kind
> of thing to make you warm

Often they will say their poems first before writing them. We share a few more ideas—about weather, my dog, snow, ice—and I send them off to the writing center to choose their paper. The excitement in the air is tangible.

I suggest that teachers supply their writing centers with all kinds of shapes and sizes of paper: long, narrow paper without lines, wide storybook paper, small, skinny pieces, large index cards, small books of all different types.

What's important is to get the children immersed in the pleasure and power of poetry. I try to give students a sense of option. They can write poems about a feeling they've had, they can try to surprise people, they can close their eyes to get a picture in their minds, they can study or observe something carefully, write a song, or write about something they've seen. They can just draw a picture, or they can try to sound out words and use invented spelling. (See Lucy Calkins, *The Art of Teaching Writing,* 1986.) They can say their poems out loud to somebody. I stay away from taking dictation, because it creates a dependency, and I'd have a line of kids waiting for me to write their poems down. I sometimes write the poems down and stick them on the back of the kids' originals, so we won't forget the words.

It's also important to remind them that they're already intimately familiar with poetry, from nursery rhymes and songs; I tell them to build on the knowledge they already have, getting started by singing songs or reading nursery rhymes. In fact, a Writing Project colleague of mine, Jim Sullivan, began poetry in his class by reading nursery rhymes first. Then the class wrote their own.

Also, in the beginning I stress rhyme and repetition much more than I do in the older grades. Particularly in kindergarten, rhyme still seems to be a new enough concept so their rhymes aren't clichéd and worn; look at this rhymed poem written by a kindergartner:

> A Big Fat Whale
> Jumped right on the girl's nail

Sometimes I read them rhyming books, like *Each Peach Pear Plum* or *Goodnight, Moon,* and they fill in the rhyme or repetition. There's a wide selection; many picture books are poems infused with all the elements of poetry: rhythm, repetition, and rhyme. Or I read them short, imagistic poems or longer, rhythmic ones like "Stopping by Woods on a Snowy Evening."

Of course, things don't always get started as nicely as they did at P.S. 176, especially if the kids have little or no experience with poetry. In one kindergarten the workshop began with a fiasco. I brought in a guitarist friend of mine, and we played and sang songs the kids knew. When it was time for them to write their poems, they were so excited, half the class sang "Rudolph the Red-Nosed Reindeer" or "Jingle Bells" or "The Itsy Bitsy Spider" as their poem even though we had stressed thinking up original poems. Often what very young kids remember becomes theirs; there is no difference between what they remember and what they make up. When I talked to them about it, the problem went away. But this is where the blank book I've already suggested the teacher set up for the class comes in handy; if the students remember poems written by somebody else, they can write them down and share them with the class, and then go back to writing their own.

Many times it seems more natural to start by reading poems to a small group of kids who are interested in writing poetry, instead of working with the entire class. Take them to a table or a special poetry place where they can learn about and write poetry; gradually the others in the class may join in. The advantage to this approach is that students don't feel pressured to write poetry; they come to it when they're ready. One drawback is that because of fear, or stereotypes about poetry, many students will never try.

There are many ways to begin a primary poetry workshop, but some key ingredients remain the same:

- Always immerse the kids in poetry first; have them bathe in it, splash in it, until you think they know poetry.
- Let them know that they can write; show them poems written by kids in kids' handwriting. Encourage "invented spelling."
- Stress the variety of topics they can write about: feelings, something they can see, things they're curious about, pictures in their minds, and so on.
- Bring in a wide variety of paper—long, narrow, wide, small—and let them choose what fits their poems best.
- For kindergarten students, I suggest that teachers begin the year with stories, to get them used to writing, but also to spend time reading poems to them. After they feel comfortable with writing in general, they're ready to begin writing poetry.
- Suggest, as one teacher did, that the kids indicate when they're writing a poem by putting a "P" at the top of the page.

Reading poetry with kindergartners and first graders

When I read aloud to kindergartners and first graders, they often move to the rhythm—they grasp a part of the poem's mystery immediately. Most of the time it's pretty obvious who likes what poem. But how do young children interpret what they're reading, what do they think? This is a difficult question for the little ones, but I have tried it, especially at the beginning of the writing workshop.

In Dora Ferraiuolo's first-grade class at P.S. 220 in Queens I gathered the children together. "One of the main things that poems have in them is pictures," I said. "Just from the words, poems sometimes give you pictures in your head. I've brought in a poem that gives me a picture in my mind.

I'm going to read it; maybe you can look in your minds and see what you see." On a chart I had written a poem I'd found:

Night settles on earth,
and the blue city becomes
a nest of fireflies.

"For today," I said, "I'd like you to choose some paper and make a drawing of what the poem looks like to you. The poem will be right here, so you can keep reading it to remind you of what it says."

They went back to their seats to draw. As the teacher and I walked around looking at their drawings, at first we were disappointed. They didn't get the poem, I thought to myself. I had always imagined it as describing New York City at night, with the tall buildings' lights lit and twinkling. That's probably what I would have drawn.

At one desk I saw a huge red nest with a city inside. The fireflies were flying out of the city. At another I saw large, yellow fireflies, a huge earth surrounded by the night . . . and suddenly I realized that I was the one who wasn't getting it. Their drawings were filled with their rich visions of the poem. It would have been so boring if anybody had done just a city at night.

As Dora and I talked with them, we kept referring to the text, line by line: " 'Night settles on earth'—where is that in your drawing?" Or we'd point to something in their drawings and ask where it was in the poem. All of them stuck to the text, yet let their imaginations fly.

When we gathered to share, they stood up next to the poem and kept referring back to it. David showed his drawing and said: "City is in the nest. Fireflies carry out of the nest. They are black because night is black. Black on side of nest is the shadow." In his drawing, the blue city had literally become a nest of fireflies, which is the central metaphor of the poem. I didn't need to say, "Do you understand that the blue city becomes a nest because the lights in the city look like fireflies?" They already knew this and added their own interpretations. In Reynold's drawing he explained, "The thunder, the electricity in the city"—he meant lightning but didn't know the word for it—"goes to the fireflies' nest. The city becomes the fireflies' nest." Reynold drew an arrow, showing us the connection, the "becoming." James didn't know what a firefly was, but he made his bug red because he knew fire was red. He took each word of the poem and drew it.

Metaphor works by making reality more complex and interesting, broadening its meaning; the students in Dora's class were responding to metaphor.

The concept of imagery had become tangible for them. My next step could have been to read other imagistic poems and have them jot down pictures in their heads and discuss them. Eventually they would have come up with their own images to write as poems.

Later, I brought in a poem whose central character was more rhythmic than imagistic. "Another thing poems make you do sometimes is what songs make you do: tap your foot or clap your hands. Here's a poem that does that." On the board I had written Eloise Greenfield's "Things" (see p. 27). As I read it, they swayed and snapped their fingers and clapped their hands. Then I asked them to pair off, go to different parts of the room, and try to make a dance or a play of the poem. At first they were shy; then one by one they got started.

At the end, as the rest of the class said the poem in unison, each pair performed it. Some people clapped to it, some acted it out, some jumped imaginary ropes to it, some danced to it. A few people, to show when the rhythm changed, switched from clapping to snapping.

When all the pairs had gone, the children knew the poem by heart. A few of them made comments.

"It made me so happy I wanted to cry at the 'still got it' part."

"It was like rock 'n' roll."

"It made me want to dance so I just did it."

Dora remarked, "This is one way to develop a love of poetry that will stay." We want to replace rigid interrogations about poems with discovery and joy. Once students find this deep pleasure in reading, they can't help having it as they write.

Conferring

My first experience with teaching poetry was in a kindergarten class in that small mountain school in New Hampshire. I had no idea what to expect. On that first day when I spoke to the kids about poetry and they began to write, I was amazed. A little girl who wrote about her grandmother who had died drew one picture of the grandmother lying on a bed and another of an apple going into a hole; I had no idea what the apple meant, but somehow, strangely, mysteriously, it seemed to relate. There was the girl who said, "Stars, stars, they're like they're brand new to me," or William, who said, "Moons, moons, I've seen too many moons." Often my response to their poems was astonishment. It still is. But it's still possible to respond to their work in various other ways. I use many of the same conferring ideas that I use with the upper grades; here are some, adapted to suit the grade level.

In Liz McGrath's kindergarten class we're walking around the room together talking to her students about their writing. First we walk over to Robert to see what he's doing. He has drawn a picture of the sun on his paper and has written some letters down. I ask him if he would mind reading his poem back to us; I'm curious to see if he will remember the poem he recited earlier, during the minilesson. He reads the poem almost exactly as he had said it before and says he's finished and is going to start another. He knows exactly what he's doing.

At the same table another Robert has a blank piece of paper in front of him, with no picture and no words on it. He looks very sad. We stoop down and talk to him.

"How's it going, Robert? Do you have any ideas for a poem?"

He looks very unhappy. He nods his head yes.

"Can you say your poem to me?"

He shakes his head no.

"Do you know what it's about?"

"The sun. It's like Robert W.'s, 'Sun oh sun . . . ' "

"Okay. Why don't we try something? Try and imagine the sun. What do you see in your mind?"

He begins slowly, his eyes shut tight. "The sun rises morning and night." Then he opens his eyes.

"Robert! Your poem is wonderful. I could see that in my mind. Now that's your poem—with *your* feelings about the sun. Okay—I'm going to visit some other kids. I'll be back. I can't wait to read it."

When I return, I am struck by the shape of Robert's poem on the page, how he has taken in the concept from the kids' poems he'd seen that day, but also from all the poems on large paper that Liz has put up around the room. (See Figure 7–3.)

In this conference, I explain to Liz, he made a breakthrough. He now knows he can write poetry. He has learned three things: the importance of looking in his own mind for ideas; the value of saying his poem to someone first, then writing it down or drawing it; and the simple fact that although poetry may be scary at first, success feels good and will inspire him to write some more.

We move on and squat down to talk to Ahmed. He has this on his paper:

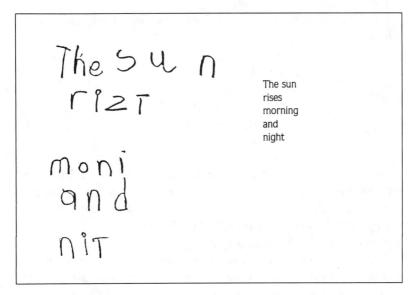

The sun
rises
morning
and
night

Figure 7–3   Robert's poem

Srrbt srr lit fr
drr I see Towlt

This translates as, "Star bright, star light, first dream I see tonight."

"It's so beautiful," I say. "I want to sing it. How did you get the idea for the poem?" I ask this question often.

"I like the nighttime," Ahmed says, " 'cause I have all these pleasant dreams."

Ahmed has taken a poem we all know but changed the words a little bit. Sometimes when kids copy poems verbatim, I say, "You know, I've heard that poem before; you could write it in the class book. But the next poem you write, I want to know what *you* think. It's you we're interested in." But in kindergarten the distinction between memory and originality is blurred.

I say, "You know, sometimes poets write a few poems about the same thing. You have this one poem about nighttime and dreams, and it seems like you have more to say; I'm wondering if you might want to write another poem about it. In fact, some poets write whole books about the same thing. They just keep saying it different ways." I give him the option to experiment or not.

Later, Ahmed shows me his second poem, stapled to the first to resemble a book:

> Night night
> I like night
> I wish night came
> every night
> like mice.

This conference with Ahmed reminded me that revision for the younger kids often takes place not on one particular poem but over several poems. I could have said to Ahmed, "You know, I'd rather you wrote your own poem," but how would that have helped him? In a conference, I try to generate a spark for the next poem they'll write.

Sometimes in a conference I don't know what to say; I just put my arm around a child and hug him. In Dora Ferraiuolo's first-grade class a little boy had said in the beginning that he was going to write about his bird who had died. When he finished his poem he came over to show it to us. (See Figure 7–4.)

The previous summer, he explained, his family shut all the windows in the house when they left; when they came back, his parrot was dead. The only response I could give him was to hug him and thank him for letting us read his poem. I also told him that this was exactly what poets do: write about things that feel urgent, things they care about.

As I mentioned earlier, young kids often say their poems to me first. One first grader, Barbara, walked up, tugged on my skirt, and said, "Ms. Heard, Ms. Heard, I have a poem!" When I asked what it was, she pointed to her head. "Do you have it in your mind?" I asked. She nodded. "I'd love to hear it," I said. Barbara stood very tall, her chin in the air, and slowly began to say her poem, measuring her words:

> Angels sing
> Hearts go away
> Butterflies die

I was astonished. I asked her to say it again. "How did you get the idea for this poem?" I asked.

"We had butterflies in the class," she said. "And then they died." She paused. "I drew a picture of it."

Hot day is a warm
day and birds
die and birds
in the ground
birds that are loved.

Figure 7–4   Jonathan's poem

I followed her to her desk, and there was the picture—an angel, some butterflies, and some hearts.

"You know, Barbara, your poem is so beautiful I'm sure everyone would like to hear it. Are you going to write some of the letters down?" She nodded but looked hesitant and scared. We sounded out the first couple of words together; it's a good idea sometimes just to sit with a child and provide support as she tries to sound out the words. After I left Barbara wrote the rest of the poem. (See Figure 7–5.)

So often what the kids say is strange, mysterious, and amazing, poetry already, and they don't know it. In one class Suzanne Gardinier was sitting at a table of first graders who wanted to write poetry, reading and talking to them about poems. She told them she was writing a poem about soot and asked if any of them knew what that was. One little girl said, "I don't know about poetry, but once my mother took us on the Brooklyn Bridge and all that dark stuff came down lightly." Suzanne said to her, "Wow! There you go; that's a poem right there. That's beautiful."

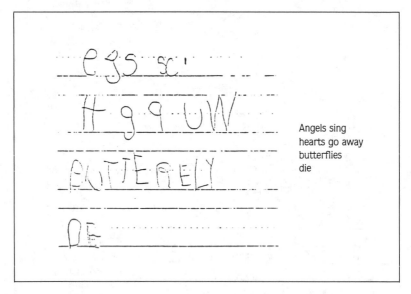

Angels sing
hearts go away
butterflies
die

Figure 7–5   Barbara's poem

If I set out to apply my conferring strategies when I'm talking to kids, I get too caught up in teaching and forget to enjoy, delight in, and feel the kids' poems. In a workshop, my goal is not to make great poems but to make sure a spark is ignited in the children—they should have fun and enjoy what they're doing. It's good to remember that not everything has to be taught in a conference.

One of the main concerns teachers have when they begin teaching poetry to their younger students is how to get kids to write poems and not stories. On that day in Liz's class, she and I knelt to talk to Mary, who had drawn a house with smoke coming out of the chimney and two figures in front of it. No letters. When I asked her to say her poem to us, she spoke in a small, shy voice: "And me and my mommy we walked to the store to buy some food, and then we came home."

To both Liz and me, this sounded like a story. I wanted to know what Mary thought. So I asked her, "Is this a poem or a story?" With hesitation, she said, "It's a poem."

"Do you know what makes it a poem?"

A hard question. She shrugged her shoulders.

I asked myself, would it help Mary to know that I think her poem seems like a story? Especially when she had already said it was a poem? It's at these

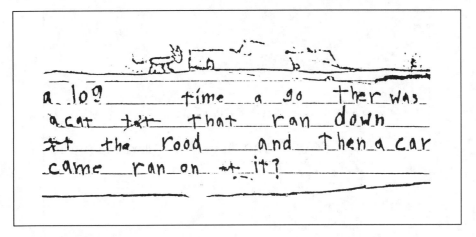

a log   time   a go   ther was
a cat tht   that   ran down
tt the rood   and Then a car
came   ran on at it?

Figure 7–6   Vincent's piece

times that it's best just to use the conference to gather information and ideas for minilessons for the whole class. Because there were several storylike poems in the class I suggested to Liz that she discuss what a poem sounds like and what a story sounds like, both in minilessons and in conferences, and that she try to teach different elements of a poem, such as repetition, strong rhythm, and rhyme, so the boundaries between prose and poetry wouldn't be so unclear.

I had a related experience in a first-grade class in Brooklyn. After the second week of writing poetry, I conferred with a student named Vincent, who had written the text shown in Figure 7–6. After Vincent read his piece to me and we talked a little about it, I asked him, "Do you think it's a poem or a story?" He looked at me and in a voice that was meant to show up my ignorance said, "A story." Of course!

"Oh, you're working on stories today?"

"Well," he said, "as soon as I finish the story, I'm going to write a poem about the same thing."

"I'm looking forward to reading it, Vincent," I said. "I'll be back."

I returned a little later, and Vincent had written the poem in Figure 7–7. Pointing to the two pages, I asked, "What makes this a story and this a poem?" He shrugged his shoulders. We tried to figure it out together so we could teach the class. "Well, it sounds different," I said. "But how?"

"The poem is shorter. The sentences are shorter."

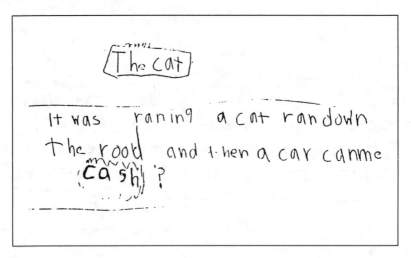

Figure 7–7   Vincent's poem, "The Cat"

"Yes, and the rhythm is quicker. There's a beat to the poem." All of this I could try to teach in a minilesson sometime.

Many of my conferences and lessons attend to this issue: what makes a poem sound the way it does? There are no quick answers, but just having the question in the air helps kids remember that poems do sound different from stories.

It's important to remember that it takes time for some students to hear the voice of poetry. Such was the case with first grader Manuel.

Manuel was finished writing. I stooped down to talk with him about his "poem" (shown in Figure 7–8).

I began, as I often do, by asking Manuel if I could read his poem back to him. I read it and asked him what he thought of it. He shrugged his shoulders.

"You know what I was wondering, Manuel? Is this a poem or a story?" I say this with real curiosity, genuinely wanting to know what Manuel's intention was for his work. "It's a story," he said.

"I was thinking about that, too. Do you want to write a poem?" He said yes.

"This happens to poets a lot," I said. "First you put your ideas down, and sometimes it starts coming out as a story. The next step is to make it more into a poem. If you were going to make this into a poem, what do you think you could do?"

Manuel shrugged.

I like my frends. I weNT to
The beach with my Frends
When I was going to The
beach. DuT ToDaY I Was
good iN The beach.
a DooT road on The WaTer
Will You go 'Pleas oKay
I will go home.

Figure 7–8   Manuel's piece

"Well, why don't you try this: close your eyes and imagine a beach. Tell me what you see in your mind. Just talk."

As he described what he saw in his mind, I wrote down what he said. "And that's all." He opened his eyes.

I showed him what I'd done and read back to him what he had said. He looked delighted. "You know, you can do that with a poem," I said. "You can imagine it in your mind and then just write the words. Why don't you get another piece of paper and try that." His second draft—or poem version—of "The Beach" is shown in Figure 7–9.

Manuel shared the two versions of his poem at the end of class and taught the other kids how they could turn their stories into poems.

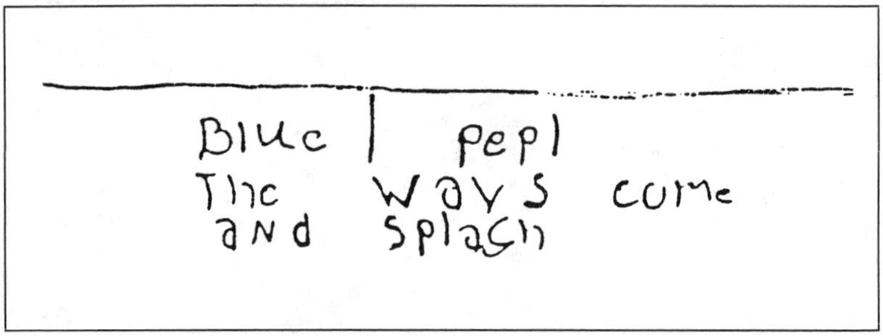

BIuc | Pepl
The waYs cume
and splash

Figure 7–9   Manuel's poem, "The Beach"

In some conferences I simply point out some of the things a student has put in a poem, maybe even without knowing it: repetition, or special words, or the poem's shape, or the way the poem is about something very important to the writer. Teachers who have watched me mention that I often say, "You do exactly what poets do." They're right; I also carry a sheet of carefully selected poems, to show students similarities between their poems and, say, Lilian Moore's or Gwendolyn Brooks's.

Later in the poetry workshop, many of my conferences tend to center around how to help students extend or shape their poems. In both kindergarten and first grade, many are thrilled just to write anything down, but especially in the first grade, when writing is easier, I've found that many kids just whip through poem after poem. Although their fluency is remarkable, I sometimes like to give them a challenge; I ask them to try to write a second stanza, to extend their thinking on the same subject. Sometimes a challenge can trigger new ideas. But it's important to remember that every writer has the option to say, "No, I'm done."

The same is true for experimenting with the shape of their poems. I might suggest in a conference that they look through a book of poems to see how other poets shape their poems, then ask them to get different-sized papers and try to write their poems again, using different shapes to see which ones they like. I encourage playfulness first, experimentation, before mentioning the line or line breaks.

Finally, I read the poems back to my students so they can hear the sound of their poems; they may imagine more images, hear something that doesn't please them and change it, or just smile a deep, rich smile when they realize that those are their words that sound so good.

Most of my minilessons for kindergarten and first grade come from what I notice around the room and from the kids' own poems. I encourage teachers to look for their own minilessons, based on the circumstances of their classrooms. Here are some examples of minilessons other teachers have done.

Liz McGrath began the writing workshop one day with all her twenty-eight kids sitting with their legs crossed in the poet's corner.

"Yesterday, when I was walking to my car," Liz began, "the wind blew, and I saw these small pieces of ice. The wind made them scatter. It sounded like glass to me. So I decided to write a poem." She said very slowly:

> Ice crystals
> shattered
> glass pieces
> scraping on the ground

She said it twice. Then she said, "I tried to use words in my poem that are unusual, words nobody ever thought of before. That's something poets think about. Today maybe you can think of interesting words, words nobody ever thought of, to describe things in a new way, in your own way."

That day Robert wrote a poem that began, "The snow is a miracle." In my conference with him I pointed out that "miracle" was a great word to use; it surprised me, it refreshed me. Poets use great words like that all the time, just like he did. Liz asked him to share his poem with the class at the end, to punctuate her minilesson. As Liz pointed out, the word "miracle" is not particularly great in itself, but used by a kindergartner in the line "The snow is a miracle," it is transformed.

Using interesting words is fundamental to poetry. I've introduced an "interesting word list" in the poet's corner; on a big piece of paper the class collects words that are fun to say or that describe something in an unusual way: words like "shattered," "scraping," or "miracle." It's important to include the kids' poems on the chart, to put the words in context.

Dora Ferraiuolo read this poem to her class again:

> Night settles on earth,
> and the blue city becomes
> a nest of fireflies.

"Do you hear that word 'settles' in this poem?" she asked. "Sometimes when you get restless, you hear me say, 'Settle down.' Well, look at this poem; the poet says, 'Night settles on earth,' just like you settling down in your seats. The poet says, 'Night *settles*'; poets choose their words so carefully. Sometimes they use words you don't expect, words that surprise us. When you're writing your poems, you might want to pick words that could surprise people."

This concept is important, and there are many ways to teach it; in Barbara Rynerson's first-grade class in Amherst, we noticed that many of the children were writing quick, one-line poems, like "The stars are beautiful like the sun." I decided to address this in a minilesson.

I wrote Langston Hughes's "April Rain Song" (see p. 26) on a large piece of paper and folded the bottom under so only the first three lines showed. After I read them these lines, I said, "Langston Hughes could have stopped here, after these three lines. But he didn't. Instead, he went on and said more. He had more things to say about the rain, so he added more to his poem. When you write your poems, you might remember that, when you think you're all done. You might want to add another stanza to your poem."

In another minilesson Dora came into her class and told her first graders that when her husband is tense or has something on his mind, he walks around reciting lines by a famous Italian poet named Dante. He had memorized the lines; he has them in his head and can say them at any time to help him relax. She suggested that if they really loved a poem or part of a poem, they might want to learn it by heart. The next day, and for days afterward, her students came into the class with a poem or part of a poem memorized and shared it with the class.

In one class of kindergarten students, I talked about how important it is for some poets to try to get a picture in their minds of what they're writing about. One poet, Randall Jarrell, wrote a poem called "A Bat Is Born," which really gave me a picture of what it's like to be a bat. I brought in the picture book *A Bat Is Born,* based on the poem, read it to them and showed them the pictures, and asked them what pictures they saw in their minds.

Another way of doing this minilesson is to read a poem and ask students to draw the pictures that the poem brings to their minds; you could discuss how everyone sees the same thing, but in a different way. It's a way to strengthen the idea of the making of imagery.

In kindergarten and first grade I usually talk about the shape of poems rather than trying to teach line breaks. I tell my students that poems are like buildings: they have different shapes and sizes. If you flip through an anthology, it's like looking at a city. One lesson I've done to discuss shape is to write poems of different shapes on a large chart, to give them options for experimenting with their own poems.

I always try to discuss the three R's with my kindergarten and first-grade students: rhythm, rhyme, and repetition. I frequently use picture books in my minilessons, because often picture books are poems or are prose that is poetic. I've used the illustrated version of Robert Frost's "Stopping by Woods on a Snowy Evening" with kindergarten classes. I don't need to say too much, except that many poems have rhythm and that they're like songs. Once a girl discovered that the rhythms of the poem were like the rhythm of the horse walking.

The one thing I try not to do is to teach too much about poetry. I've found that my students learn so much more than what I tell them, just by osmosis.

Bringing the world into poetry

About two weeks into the poetry workshop in Dora Ferraiuolo's class, Dora and I walked around the room trying to get a sense of what was going on in the class. Dora noticed that many of her students were writing poems about rainbows, unicorns, or colors, poems that were definitely not stories but that didn't have much to do with what was going on in their lives. Their topics seemed very limited; so did the words they were using. The language didn't have that originality that characterizes poetry. Where was the poem about Manuel's bird? Or Michele's cat who died? They'd talked about these events in sharing that day, but they were nowhere to be found in the poems.

I realized that maybe they didn't know that they could bring their worlds into their poems—that they could write about what they were curious about, what they were concerned about, what they had seen on their way to school. Maybe they hadn't heard poems about these things. This got me thinking about how to encourage and nurture this worldliness in poems.

In one class in Queens, students' poems started to broaden because the environment changed. In the back of the classroom one teacher set up a science center. In it she put a petrified bug, a butterfly, leaves, a branch of pussy willow, and empty yogurt cups with various smells in them, such as garlic. All over the walls of the center were poems about things in the world: an apple, clouds, an oil slick, a butterfly. There was also a book labeled "Observations and Questions" where the kids could write any questions or comments they had about what was on the table or what was on their minds.

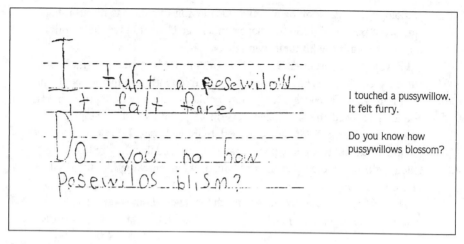

I touched a pussywillow.
It felt furry.

Do you know how
pussywillows blossom?

Figure 7–10　Lauren's piece

They could even write poems. One piece written there was about the pussy willow. (See Figure 7–10.) Lauren's piece isn't a poem, but the authentic voice in the questions sounds like the seed of a poem. Questions and curiosity are the sparks that set poems off.

It's important to create an environment where asking questions is nurtured. In one first-grade room there was a chart titled "Air Questions":

1. What are some things that have air inside?
2. What are some things that go up in air?

Then there was a list of "What Air Does," divided into two categories:

Moves	Doesn't Move
paper	cars
feathers	benches

This age group lives in a whole other world. In no other grade would you find a list like this. In sixth grade, there are lists like "What Is a Paragraph" or "Prepositions." It's as if after first grade many kids are no longer allowed to ask questions, as if they aren't supposed to wonder about the world anymore.

Dora once put a Carl Sandburg poem up on the wall near the weather chart. It began "The fog comes in on little cat feet." It was a foggy day; the class could barely see the Long Island Expressway overpass that lies directly under the window. During writing time, many students decided they wanted to write their own poems about the fog, to put up beside Sandburg's poem. Some of them stood at the window with their papers and markers, looking out into the fog. Two of their poems are shown in Figures 7–11 and 7–12.

Dora put these and other poems they wrote about the weather all around the weather center.

When my colleague Jim Sullivan taught first grade in Amherst, he planned a course of study called "Sky Awareness." When the kids in his class were studying clouds, Jim also read them poems about clouds. He was marinating them in poetry even before they wrote poems, reading them poetry about the world.

So much of the delight teachers feel when they teach kindergarten and first grade is born of the kids' natural curiosity, their everyday discoveries and transformations, their original way of looking at the world. Poets have the same curiosity; much of the process of writing poetry consists of thorough and accurate observation. I decided to experiment with this over a few days in Barbara Rynerson's class, where the kids had been writing poems for a while. I brought an apple to class and cut it in half; then I read the poem "Apple" (p. 66). I talked about how Nan Fry had had to look at an apple really hard in order to write that poem. That's what poets do; they observe things with great intensity, which makes their poems seem true.

Over the next few days in the class, some kids chose to observe things to write poems about. Sarah stood by the chick incubator and stared at the eggs inside. She later wrote the poem in Figure 7–13. When I asked what she meant when she said, "How they sparkle to begin," she told me that every morning somebody has to spray the eggs, to keep them moist so they'll hatch; when they're sprayed, they sparkle.

A few kids took the plants they were growing off the windowsill and put them on the table in front of them. It was wonderful to see kids touching and smelling and looking at plants, then intermittently writing down their thoughts and observations. Talya and Damien wrote the poems in Figures 7–14 and 7–15.

Not everyone wrote about what they observed in the world; some wrote about their families, or a dog, or any of a hundred other topics. A rich variety of poems emerged from this classroom, poems about feelings and poems about the world.

FOg

FOg is sneald

and quiet

like a river

Fog is sneaky
and quiet
like a river

Figure 7–11 "Fog"

Figure 7–12 Another poem about fog

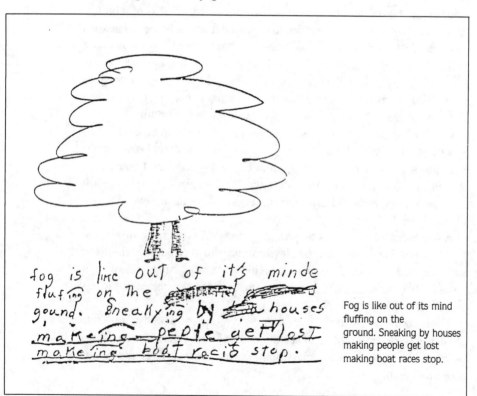

fog is line out of it's minde
flufing on the
gound. Sneaking by houses
makeing pepte get lost
makeing boat racio stop.

Fog is like out of its mind
fluffing on the
ground. Sneaking by houses
making people get lost
making boat races stop.

Eggs are brown or white
How they sparkle to begin
When they sparkle
they make my wish come true.

Figure 7–13   "White Eggs" by Sarah

Toward the end of my residency in the Campton School, I put together a small booklet of poems written by the kindergarten students; I photocopied a few extra sets and gave them to some of my friends. I gave one to a good friend, Marie Howe, a poet, whose book was recently chosen for publication by the National Poetry Series. Later she called and thanked me; she said the book was one of the best collections on contemporary poetry she had read in years.

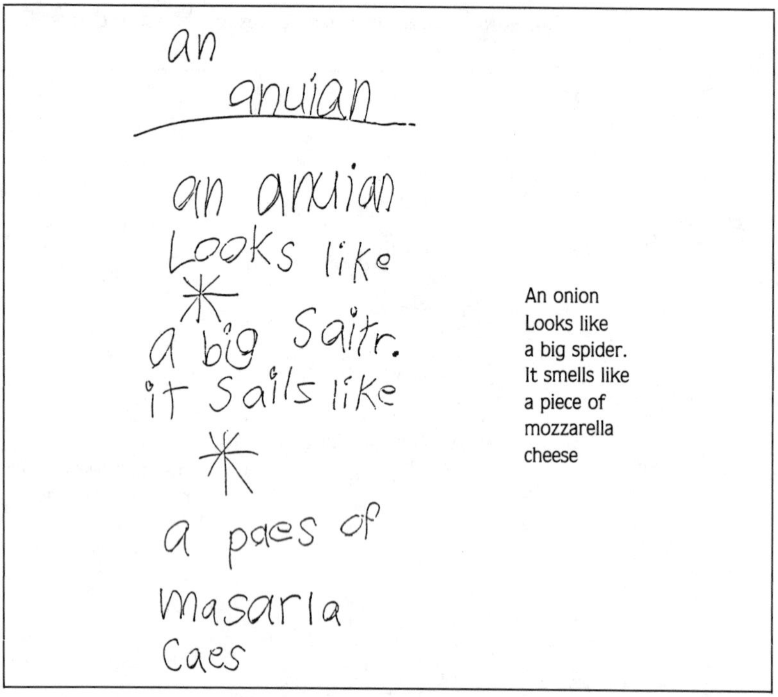

an

anuian

an anuian
Looks like

a big Saitr.
it Sails like

a paes of

masarla
Caes

An onion
Looks like
a big spider.
It smells like
a piece of
mozzarella
cheese

Figure 7–14   *"An Onion" by Talya*

Figure 7–15   *"Leaves" by Damien*

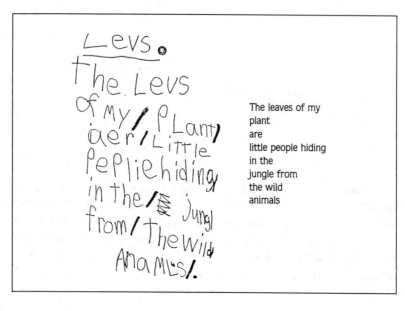

Levs.
The Levs
of my / PLant)
aer / Little
PePliehiding
in the / Jungl
from / the wild
AnaMl·s/.

The leaves of my
plant
are
little people hiding
in the
jungle from
the wild
animals

8
Making a World of Poetry: Rituals

During one of my visits to Amherst, Massachusetts, I made an appointment to visit Emily Dickinson's house. I'd driven by it many times, trying to guess which window had been hers, trying to feel her spirit there. As I walked around the house in the late afternoon, guided by two elderly women, I tried to imagine Emily in her living room, or at the piano, or walking across her room upstairs.

The tour's main event was the poet's bedroom, where she eventually spent almost all her time and wrote many of her poems. The other visitors and I were very eager to see this room, as if it would give us a clue to Emily herself; when we finally entered, we looked around intently. The guide explained that the small table near the window was not the one Emily used to write on but was exactly like it; the stove was similar to the one she had used; so was the chest of drawers. The bed she had slept in was there and, enclosed in a glass case, a dress she actually had worn. We all examined it carefully. Probably the most interesting things in her room were three lithographs on the wall: one of Carlisle, one of George Eliot, and one of the Brontë sisters. I tried to picture the trees outside her room as they had been a century ago, half as big, and the main road, then a dirt path; I wondered what she had seen from her window, how she had moved, how her face had looked when she was writing.

There were very few genuine artifacts in the house; very little of it was as it had been when Emily Dickinson lived in it. But even seeing the little there was made me feel closer to her and to her poems.

Before I left to drive back to New York, I bought a photograph postcard, a facsimile of one of Dickinson's poems. When I got home I taped it to the wall in front of my desk, next to the photographs of poets who've been important to my life. Also on the wall are poems I love, books on shelves, and quotes about writing and about living one's life in a brave way.

Where I write, and the rituals I create for myself there, are crucial to keeping the writing spirit alive in me. The maps in my apartment, the hundreds of books, the teas, the photographs of writers and poets, and the quotes on the walls all create a richness that nourishes my writing. Somehow seeing Emily Dickinson's house became part of that richness. I saw how another writer did it, how she lived, what helped her survive and flourish.

This kind of lush richness is also of the utmost importance in classrooms where poetry is being written and read. Nivea Alvarez's classroom at P.S. 148 in Queens reminded me of a flower garden in summer—brilliant colors, constant motion, and the humming not of bees but of her students reading and writing poems. The rituals and arrangements that Nivea had set up contributed to this richness. Each student had her own colorful poetry folder, where all her poems were kept. (It's important that poetry be given a special place of its own, not just mixed in with other writing or assignments.) Also, each student had a small spiral notebook in which to copy down favorite poems or to jot down ideas or the kernels of a poem. The students often brought their notebooks to the sharing time at the end of the writing workshop. Many teachers bring in a photograph album in which to collect students' favorite poems. In many rooms, as in Nivea's, there is a place where all the poetry books are kept, along with individual copies of poems that the students bring in.

One of the most interesting rituals Nivea invented was a writers' quote chart. It started with a minilesson I gave on how writers love to talk about writing, what they've learned from it, what it means to them. The quotes on my apartment walls nurture me in the morning as I'm brushing my teeth, before a day of writing or a day of work. They give me courage. Why not bring that force into the classroom?

Nivea, inspired by a teacher in upstate New York, wrote a Wallace Stevens quote, "A poem refreshes the world," on a large piece of paper and hung it on the wall. The class talked about what they thought it meant and whether or not it was true. Nivea then suggested that if any of them thought of an idea about poetry or read a line that inspired them to think about poems, they could write it down next to Stevens's words. Over the course of the month, the paper filled up with different colors and different handwriting, and more pieces of paper had to go up next to it. Many of these quotes became sources for minilessons, as they often taught some essential truth about poetry.

Whenever visitors spent time in Nivea's class, they would feel this richness, the variety of activities. Some kids would be writing their own poems, some reading poetry books; others would be copying favorite poems into notebooks or memorizing something. A few would be sitting in the poetry corner, writing or thinking or reading to a friend. All would be busy, nurturing their spirits with different aspects of loving poetry. That love shone in her class.

When I walked into Lynne Cohen's class in P.S. 176 in Queens I recognized the richness there as well. Lynne and I talked for a while before the workshop, and I told her about this richness I sometimes feel in classrooms, the garden atmosphere. We stood watching for a while, trying to understand what exactly made it exist.

In the back of the room was a poetry listening center: a tape recorder and blank cassettes and tapes of poets reading their poems. A few students huddled around the machine listening to poets read.

The listening center began after one of Lynne's students walked up and wanted to read her poems. She started to read quickly, not pausing at the line breaks. It was a beautiful poem, and I wondered if she had given any thought to listening to it in order to be able to read it well. It's sometimes important for me to hear my poems read, without seeing the words; it often helps with revision. That's when Lynne set up the listening center. Poetry is meant to be read aloud, to be heard; often students read their poems so quickly and in such soft voices that no one can hear them; it undervalues what they have to say. Lynne and I also thought it would be helpful for her students to listen to poets reading their poems. Her students seemed fascinated by the recordings, not just by the poems themselves but by how the poets read.

In centers like this it's also helpful to keep on hand some written copies of the recorded poems, so students can follow the text to see how the poem is shaped and where the lines are broken. A tape of a class reading or a tape of one poet in the class who wanted to publish his poems by reading them out loud might be good to include, too.

Around the room were also several computers, where students sat revising their poems, shifting the line breaks, deleting tired words, looking up new words in the thesaurus. On the walls and outside on the bulletin board hung posters students had made of poems they liked, their own and others from books they had read, so they could look up during the day and read the poems over again. Some were sitting quietly at their desks reading through anthologies. Later we asked Tamika what she'd been reading; she said she was trying to find out how poets title their poems. Some were simply writing.

Many rooms have a poetry corner, a place where poetry books, poems, and quotes are kept, where students can read or write poems. Lynne's poetry corner included books, student poems, and poems she had written.

The children in Lynne's room were like thirty gardeners earnestly tending the soil, each caring for a different flower. It seemed as if all the flowers were going to bloom.

I suppose my desk and the surrounding area are my poetry corner; but throughout the apartment I display information I've collected about poets and writers. Each time I go to my desk I read the draft of the Dickinson poem I bought at her house; it's important to me to know what Walt Whitman looked like, how he lived.

I suggest that each classroom have a section of biographies of poets and writers. By studying poets' lives, a poet learns herself how to live. As one poet says, that kind of information "enlarges the sense of the possible."

Photographs are also important. Many students have no idea what poets look like; seeing a photograph of one of their favorites makes poetry more real to them. I think many students think that all poets are dead or somehow of a different world; to know that they look like regular people makes what they do more familiar.

There are many ways students can begin to know particular poets. In her first-grade class in Queens, Dora Ferraiuolo devoted an entire bulletin board to celebrating Langston Hughes's birthday in February. The board was complete with a paper cake and candles, a photograph of Hughes, and several of his poems. A class could feature a different poet every week, getting to know why Nikki Giovanni punctuates the way she does or conducting a study on Gwendolyn Brooks, either as a class or in small groups. It's exciting for students to get to know a poet's work and life, to answer questions and be known as the expert on that poet. I keep files on many poets who have been important to me; anything I read about them that sounds interesting goes into the file. Teachers could collect study files on particular poets in the class.

At the checkout counter at the Putnam Valley school library in Putnam Valley, New York, the librarian set up a rotating bin with slots, each containing copies of a different poem for the children to take away with them. Every time I go there I see children spinning the bin and taking poems; I always check to see what new poems are being dispensed.

This can be done in classrooms; a teacher could have a bin of new poems each week or a box where students can drop off their favorite poems to be copied. I've also seen separate bins for different topics, labeled "deep-feeling poems" or "nature poems," "poems with strong images" or "poems about everyday things." One might hold poems that use interesting words or that use white space in an unusual way or that have unique titles. I encourage students to help me hunt for particular kinds of poems.

When I started to write poems, I used the opportunity of family birthdays to compose, then gave the poems as gifts; working under these pleasant deadlines often imbued the writing with a sense of urgency and significance. Many poems are written in honor of important occasions: a wedding, a baby's birth, a death, a birthday, a graduation. In classrooms, teachers can make blank cards and include them with regular paper in case someone chooses to write a poem for a specific occasion.

Some poetry rituals can spread beyond individual classrooms; Shelley Harwayne tells the story of one school where the teacher warned her that she had to have a poem in her pocket when she arrived. That March was poetry month, and everyone had to carry a poem.

Making anthologies

For years I taught poetry by bringing in student poems I loved and reading them to the class. In addition to the pleasure of reading the poems, I had so much fun collecting them, spending hours mulling over books, copying poems into my notebook. After reading Flora Arnstein's *Children Write Poetry* (1967), I decided I would try having my students make their own anthologies.

In many classes, as in Flora Arnstein's book, this project is done before the students even begin to write poetry, as a way for them to establish a relationship with it and to learn its varied styles and voices. In Felicia Gonsalves's fifth-grade class, the making of anthologies became a five-week project, in conjunction with the students' writing of poetry.

I began by talking to her students about what an anthologist is. Paul Janeczko, the anthologist, likens collecting poems to collecting baseball cards, which he did as a kid. He says, "I've come to read poetry the way some people watch soap operas, work in their gardens, or follow the Red Sox: irrationally, compulsively, endlessly. I read poems nearly every day whenever I find myself with a few unfilled minutes." To begin an anthology students, too, have to have a collection of favorite poems. Sometimes I ask each student to bring in large index cards on which to write poems they like, along with an envelope to keep the cards in.

Felicia had a large collection of her own books supplemented by the school library; she also put poems she had collected over the years in a poetry book of her own. We tried to offer the kids as much variety as possible, not just rhyming poems.

After introducing the concept of anthology making we talked about how to collect poems. Many students were used to reading so quickly that the deeper and more difficult poems were being passed over. Some also still thought all poetry had to rhyme and so automatically went to those poems first. We handed out a sheet of poems written by different poets. I read the poems to them and talked about variety. "Some are like stories," I said, "some rhyme, some are 'deep-feeling poems,' some require you to read them more than once or twice. It's important to read all kinds of poems and to try to leave yourself open to variety as you're collecting—don't go automatically to the ones that rhyme. Try to open your mind first."

On another day we talked about what happens when you find a poem you don't understand. "Some poetry is like that," I said. "You just don't get it until after four readings." I suggested they read the poem once silently, then again out loud. Then they might look up any unfamiliar words and afterward have a friend read it aloud slowly one more time.

Sometimes working with a partner, talking, will help to understand the poem. "If it's a poem that moves you," I said, "even though you don't quite understand it, put it away for a while. Carry it around with you. Pull it out during the day to see if anything has become clearer. Write down questions in your reading log; each day at the end of reading the class can have a share time to talk about the poems. People could discuss questions then."

Many of the teachers I work with use this writing workshop format, beginning with a short minilesson, then moving on to conferences, and ending with a sharing time. Felicia found this structure helpful in her reading classroom.

For weeks, the children collected their poems. At first, Felicia and I were skeptical. "They'll never be able to sustain the reading for five weeks," we said. But each day I'd walk in, and the kids would choose their books and begin to read. Forty-five minutes later they'd still be buried in their books. The classroom looked like a library on a Saturday afternoon.

After her students collected for a week or so, I talked to them more about the making of an anthology. I urged them to read through the poems and begin to look for connections. In an anthology, I explained, poems must connect with other poems; there must be a thread. Sometimes the connections are obvious—"nature poems" or "animal poems." Other times the connection is less apparent, as with "poems that make you feel happy."

That day they spread their index cards on tables and the floor and started to look for the threads. From then on, they began to select poems with their threads in mind, choosing what would fit into their anthologies.

The author Susan Sontag says, "The function of an anthology is to represent a world." People need to feel that the world makes sense: the seasons have patterns, day leads to night and night to day—things have an order; they're not completely random. Anthologists don't just throw things together: they make a world.

Felicia and I talked to her students about the many possible worlds they could make in an anthology.

- Some anthologies are organized around a single theme, like love or grandparents. Others have several subtopics within one unifying theme, such as the seasons, nature, or animals.
- Some anthologies are organized around form, such as Paul Janeczko's *Pocket Poems* (1985). Some collect a particular genre, such as light verse or narrative poems.
- Some anthologists collect their favorite poems by one author.
- Some are based on race, religion, or gender, like collections of poems by black or Jewish poets or by women.
- Some are just eclectic collections of favorites.

When the connections began to become clearer, we talked about how anthologies are organized. Some are divided into sections according to theme, some are arranged chronologically, some are just collections of poems without any divisions at all. I also explained the role of the introductions: it's a way for the anthologist to shake hands with the audience, to introduce herself. Introductions vary widely, but many contain a discussion

of ways to read the poems in the book; a poem that explains and introduces
the book; thoughts on how to read poetry in general; an explanation of how
and why the poems were collected; and/or a discussion of how the anthologist feels about poetry.

Each student wrote an introduction that reflected how much thought had
gone into the reading of the poems. Edgar wrote:

> Poetry is like a beautiful portrait of the Garden of Eden but in words. But
> other poems are like watching a comedy show but with no pictures. Love
> poems are like soap operas. Like in love poems they have strong emo-
> tional feeling like in t.v. programs. So I think of poems like t.v. pro-
> grams. America's family past time but no moving pictures.

Andrew wrote:

> These poems will touch your soul.
> These poems will enter your mind and never be forgotten.
> These simple words will always be with you.

We also discussed titles, dedications, illustrations, tables of contents, and
indexes. At the end of the five weeks the anthologies were typed up and read
in a celebration.

During the project I was struck by how integrated the writing and reading
were. The students truly found the connection here. We started by having
separate times for writing and reading, first reading for forty-five minutes,
then writing for forty-five minutes. During the last few weeks, though, students did both at once. Some would begin to read, then take out folders to
work on poems, books open beside them. The room held twenty-seven poets
at work, eagerly writing and reading poetry at whatever pace they chose.

As the weeks passed, I began to notice how their tastes and styles were
reflected not only in their anthologies but in their writing as well. Andrew,
who was collecting "deep-feeling poems," started to write similar poems;
Stephen both collected and wrote "nonsense" verse. My conferences with
them changed; I began to know them as writers and readers, their prefer-
ences and their tastes. For example, when I asked Stephen what made him
choose nonsense poems, he told me that his cousin had just died; he wanted
to make people laugh. "When I play games," he said, "I don't read the
directions first. I just play the game. Or when I'm walking down the halls,
I just walk. I don't notice the kids, the walls. That's how I read and write
poetry. I don't think too much about them."

Throughout the project Felicia noticed there was a deep sense of urgency and purpose in the room. It's that kind of self-directed involvement in literature that will make students read poetry all their lives.

Author's studies

My reading is always marked by periods where I read and study one particular poet. In addition to the poet's work, I like to find out about her life: how and why she wrote, how she lived, how the world did or did not receive her. The Brazilian educator Paulo Freire writes in *A Pedagogy for Liberation* (1987), "I say that reading is not just to walk on the words, and it is not flying over the words either. Reading is to discover the connections between the text and the context of the text, and also to connect the text/context with my context, the context of the reader." I form a different kind of relationship with the poetry once I've gathered this contextual information; over the years I return to those poets as I do to friends. Part of being a reader of poetry is getting to know poets and their poetry intimately. I try to encourage this in the schools.

In Debbie Davis's second-grade class and Toby Cassuto's fifth-grade class I facilitated an author study on Langston Hughes. Many of the kids already knew and loved his poetry, so we were off to a good start. To help things along, I picked out about ten poems from Hughes's *Selected Poems* and copied them to hand out; I also copied a photograph of him and collected some biographical material.

First, I read the kids many of his poems out loud, just to give them a flavor of who he is as a poet. Then I passed out his famous "Mother to Son," for us to read and discuss in more depth. I read the poem out loud, then a few people asked if they could, too.

Mother to Son

Well, son, I'll tell you:
Life for me ain't been no crystal stair.
It's had tacks in it,
And splinters,
And boards torn up,
And places with no carpet on the floor—
Bare.

But all the time
I'se been a-climbin' on,
And reachin' landin's,
And turnin' corners,
And sometimes goin' in the dark
Where there ain't been no light.
So boy, don't you turn back.
Don't you set down on the steps
'Cause you finds it's kinder hard.
Don't you fall now—
For I'se still goin', honey,
I'se still climbin',
And life for me ain't been no crystal stair.

The second graders asked some basic questions, like "What is a crystal?" Once we'd cleared that up, I asked them to go back to their seats and write in their reading notebooks. What did they notice about the poem? What did they like about it? Any general comments? What, if anything, did the poem remind them of? Did they have any questions? Was there anything they didn't understand?

As Debbie and I walked around the room, her students seemed confused. Some of them took the metaphor of the crystal stair literally at first. One said, "They live in a broken-down house and they don't have money to fix it." Someone else wrote, "She is trying to say that his life wasn't perfect. She's trying to say that life won't be easy for you if you see an ad in the newspaper and they talk about a beautiful house and you go see it and it's a torn down house. It won't be easy." Even when taking the poem literally, they understood part of its message.

In my conferences I kept asking about the crystal stair metaphor: "What does it mean?" One by one, people started popping up with their revelations, their interpretations of the poem. One boy wrote in his notebook, "The poem is ununderstandable but once you get involved and ask someone for a few ideas, it gets unconfusing . . . it's how confusing poems come to you. It's hard to live a life with no food and a crushed down house for living. She will not survive long. She wished for a good life. Maybe she'll have it if she survives long enough."

After they had finished writing, we all assembled for a sharing of ideas and questions. A few read from their notebooks to the rest of the class.

One question was, "Why did the mother write a poem to the son if he's right there?"

Some of the answers were:

"Because maybe she really loves him, cares about him, and needs to warn him."

"Maybe it's like a letter to him. Some poets write letters to people who aren't there."

These questions about the poem started a discussion that was so rich, I never had to ask the teacher's questions—the students got so excited, their own questions generated the discussion.

Another student asked, "What's she been climbing on?"

Some of the answers were: "the stairs," "the broken stairs," "they're like her torn-up life," "she can't survive," "she's hungry."

The fifth graders found the poem easier to understand. One boy remarked at the share time: "I think this was about segregation in the south. The crystal stair is like in cartoons when they get dollar signs in their eyes. She doesn't get those. She looks all over and doesn't see a crystal stair mansion. She sees what she doesn't like—she doesn't like her life—but she still goes on."

Somebody else said: "This poem and a lot of his others express about slavery—how it feels to be a slave. Everywhere you look—you can't be happy. You can't sell living things."

Even though they knew the date of the poem and they knew about civil rights, I think it was difficult for these mostly white kids to understand that racial oppression still exists. During the week, when I wasn't there, the teachers discussed the civil rights movement and the time of Langston Hughes's writing, which put his poems more in context.

The next week I brought in another Langston Hughes poem:

I, Too

I, too, sing America.
I am the darker brother.
They send me to eat in the kitchen
When company comes,
But I laugh,
And eat well,
And grow strong.

> Tomorrow,
> I'll be at the table
> When company comes.
> Nobody'll dare
> Say to me,
> "Eat in the kitchen,"
> Then.
>
> Besides,
> They'll see how beautiful I am
> And be ashamed—
>
> I, too, am America.

In Debbie Davis's second grade, their response flooded out: "Why do they send him to the kitchen?"

"Maybe he's being punished. I think it's not right because they're brothers—why should he have to sit in the kitchen?"

"He is a person, he wants to be a part of things."

They understood the gist of the poem—that something unfair was happening—but they didn't know why. Without the poem's context it was hard to understand its full meaning.

In their logs some kids wrote, "Why did he say he was the darker brother?" Then they began to understand. "He's black." "He's being put in the kitchen because he's black."

One boy said, "Maybe he's like Martin Luther King—they don't like him because he's black. Maybe he is Martin Luther King."

Michelle said, "I think it's not right that the darker brother gets to sit in the kitchen. If they're family they should love each other like brothers do. And I think it doesn't matter what color the brother is as long as they love each other."

Later someone asked, "What does he mean when says, 'I, too, sing America'?"

Someone answered, "He wants to be part of things—part of the American family."

As the study of Langston Hughes's poetry deepened, so did the students' understanding of what Hughes wrote about and the context of his poems. Someone said, "Langston Hughes expresses things with affection." Someone else said, "He talks a lot about life." What could have been an empty, formal discussion ended up filled with the richness of the world. It was begun and sustained by the students asking questions and groping for ways to answer them.

On a recent trip to Amherst, the teachers and I sat over coffee in the afternoon brainstorming ways we could celebrate poetry. We decided to have a poetry festival; each class could participate in whatever way it wished. As the afternoon wore on, we were sometimes in hysterics, coming up with all kinds of wild ways to say "yes" to poetry, to affirm all the work, progress, and joy the teachers and students had found. Here are some thoughts from that creative afternoon.

One teacher wanted his class to write postcard poems. Students could send them to people in the class.

Another class wanted to sponsor a coffee house, complete with hot chocolate, music, and poetry readings. Still another wanted to make "poetic T-shirts," with each student writing a favorite line on a shirt and wearing it to school that day. Some classes wanted to have a straight poetry reading, with a microphone, refreshments, and a tape recording made to be kept in the library. Others wanted to perform a choral reading; they'd be called the poet minstrels and travel from class to class performing. Another class wanted to make broadsheets or cards of their poems and hand them out around the school, as many poets used to do in the sixties and some do still. One class wanted to make bookmarks and bookplates and put them in the library.

The more we talked the wilder we got. A few teachers mentioned putting poems in helium balloons and sending them up into the sky, wondering who would eventually find and read them. Some wanted a poetry picnic, with a poem in each basket, or a poetry picket line. My favorite was the poetry parade: a traveling parade of students with poems on banners, some dressed as Dickinson or Frost, would roam the school, singing. It was getting late.

Planning a final celebration felt like an important ritual; we did not want to say good-bye to poetry but to celebrate the joy it had brought to the school. At the end of the semester in my graduate workshop at Teachers College, we always have a reading, an evening to celebrate poems and what we've gone through together as a class. Each student is required to put together a small chapbook of poems to hand out to everyone else.

Rituals are a way to create habits and traditions; they remove the burden of starting the process of teaching or writing poetry from scratch every day. Mostly I try not to impose too many projects on a class and to leave plenty of room for individual variations. But creating rituals that help nourish a love of poetry instead of constrict it is one of the most valuable ways a teacher can bring the rich world of the poet—like the world of Emily Dickinson's upstairs room—into the classroom.

The information, the learning, and the struggles are important in a poetry workshop, but the arrangements one makes to celebrate the harvest are just as important as nurturing the garden into bloom.

Appendix

ANTHOLOGY OF POEMS BY CHILDREN

Frogs in the Night   ADAM ENGLISH, GRADE 2

Frogs hopping hopping up and
down all around. Hear the rabbit at
night while my father
washes dishes.
My sister sits at the table
refusing to eat.
And I am happy
listening to that sweet
sound of those few
frogs in the night.

Birds   LISA EDMOND, GRADE 4

Birds are wonderful.
They fly in the sky.
Fluttering their wings in the cool breeze.
There are big white birds
that are wild and free
gliding over the cities and towns,
watching the people ride their bikes
and driving their cars.
To the birds flying in the air,
it's just like us
when we were first born
when we didn't know what was going
to happen but that there was
something wonderful coming this way.

My Cat Jimmy   FABIOLA MONDACA, GRADE 4

Jimmy died long
ago.
I still have feelings
as if Jimmy
was in the
room with me.

When I used to
hold him
I had a
feeling that he
would never
go away.

The Victory Bread   HASUN, GRADE 6

Three blue birds
Were at my window
Fighting for a piece of bread.

I ran to the kitchen
Got two pieces of bread.
I went to the window

Two were dead.
And one lay on the bread.
The two had died in a fight

For an old piece of stale bread.
The winner lay there
Closed eye and bare
On the Victory Bread!

The Imagination Whale   STEVE PERRIER, GRADE 3

The way it moved
was like a dolphin
playing in the sea.
It splashed in the
water like a building
diving down. This
whale of memories
is like a dream
come true.

Butterflies   CHARLETTE HAMAMGIAN, GRADE 1

Butterflies are like the
    letter "w."
The "w" flies into words like
    "words."
And the "w" makes the words
    like "words"
Look beautiful.

Untitled   SEKOU BOURNE, GRADE 4

The drops of rain can make a seedling grow.
And water gives us life.
But there's one thing I don't understand.
When I give my cat a bath why
does she run away?

Untitled   ELLEN CATCH, KINDERGARTEN

Tigers lay in flower beds,
Dead until the sun rises.

Spider   ERIC CHIANG, GRADE 1

Spider
Eight legs
Eight eyes
look for your dinner
A fly is passing by
Swing your web
Eat the fly
Apart

Butterflies   TANYA, KINDERGARTEN

three butterflies
flap their wings
long
skinny
tongues
licking sugar water

Hermosa Mariposa   MIGUEL, GRADE 3

Hermosa Mariposa
eres
como una rosa
y tienes los colores
de la rosa
y eres
suave como una
rosa

Coral   JESSE D. WEISS, GRADE 3

Water going in and out.
It looks like rotten wood
with holes in it.

Going in, going out.

When it's in the water
it looks like tree branches.

Going in, going out.

It's slimy.

Going in, going out.

It can be white, green, brown, yellow.

Going in, going out.

All day, all week.

Going in, going out.

It smells like sea salt.

Going in, going out.

The Night Sky CHRIS WILLIAMSON, GRADE 5

Night settles on the earth,
Then the sun is lost from our sight,
To the west side.
And the sky turns on many lights.

Millions of stars entangle with each other,
To create magical patterns,
And the moon sheds another face.

Early Morning SYBIL NEURINGER, GRADE 4

Early Morning,
the moon
still up,
three thin stars,
a cherry tree
and a mountain
top. The green,
green grass needs cutting,
the world spinning and,
little Karen swinging on
the swingset, on such a
beautiful, beautiful day.

Rain Drops   JENNY, GRADE 5

DRIP
DROP

The rain drips from the faucet in the sky as it falls
it spreads water like a wheel turning fast on a smooth
black road

PLIP
PLOP

as the rain hits the soil it sinks deep down
and pushes the flowers from the death cage

Underground

The Ocean   ANNIE NI, GRADE 4

Rushing, crashing
overhead.
    Waiting, waiting
to carry you away to
its home.
    The ocean swings
you around in its arms
    again and again.

Swinging you to sleep.

Roses   CHARLETTE HAMAMGIAN, GRADE 1

Roses are like a red, smelly
   letter "o."
That is in the word "oh."
When the letter "o" is in
   a word,
That word smells like a rose.

Forgotten ERIK METZDORF, GRADE 9

Long,
brown hair
cascades
over her shoulders.
Shoulders over-burdened
with duty,
or maybe guilt.

I see her face,
pale and tight
with lines of exhaustion
etched in patterns
like artwork.

Her beautiful hair
tied
in an ugly
ball
on the back of her head.

Through gentle wisps of hair,
I see
my mother.

Life and Death   THOMAS GILBERT, GRADE 2

Life and death.
That's what happened with
          my uncle.

He had blue eyes
Black hair
And always wore
          red socks.

It was a dark and stormy night.
A motorcycle hit
          his car.

He lived until he was twenty,
He died when he was twenty.
And that was the end
          of that.

The Answers of Stupid Questions   JUSTIN BARBARA, GRADE 2

Hi, dear. Where have you been dear?
What did you do today in school dear?
What did you do in reading dear?
What did you do in math dear?
How did you do walking home today dear?

I did good.
I did good.
I did good.
I did good.
I did good.
I did good.

Does that answer, hey Mom!
Yes, dear.

I Love Somebody RANETTA, GRADE 2

I love somebody, I know
he is black. He loves me too.
I love, he loves something.

He is in California. I am in New York.
We are not close together.
He is my dad.

My Grandpa YASSER TATARI, GRADE 3

In the small blue room stood my grandfather,
hungry and sleepy. I go to the warm kitchen
and give him the nice cup of hot tea and two toasts.
In the shallow water walks my grandpa.
He watched the animals swim a long time
ago when I was a small kid. I stood
in a blue room with my grandpa. He talked
to me. My grandpa had gone to bed.
The old wooden room was cool.
I got a nice warm blanket and
put it on him. I turned off the
pretty lantern. I kissed him and
slept in the cozy wooden room.
In the beautiful morning I made my
grandpa a nice hot breakfast.
I ate with him and helped him
out of bed and helped for
the whole day.

Mother's Arms   LESA BROWN, GRADE 8

It's a place with all the comforts
of home.
It's the first place I run to
when there's no other place to go.
It shows me when I'm feeling
low that it will always be there.
It helped me through the roughest
time I ever want to be in.
It's the safest place I know.
But why does it have to hold on
so tight?

My Dad   ANNIE NWOKOYE, GRADE 5

First a secure knot.
Me at one end,
my dad at the other. Slowly
something is cutting away at the knot and
it finally breaks. All is lost.
There the war begins,
fighting to stay together.
The knot is safely tied,
but every once in awhile. . . .

Pony Tail   AMY SARDINAS, GRADE 1

Pony tails
are my favorite
cause when my mom
made me a pony tail
it hurt a lot.
She said it hurts
to be beautiful.

Who I Care About   LEMONIA, GRADE 3

> I care about god
> I care about old people
> and I care about my family
> I care about Jesus is my best
> grandfather. God is my best father
> because my father died.

Her   GINA COLANTUONI, GRADE 8

> She was big and fat
> with a child inside.
>
> I was hoping it would be a girl.
> After all I had three brothers.
>
> And it was a girl,
> small and dainty,
> but two months too early.
> Here I was with a sister, finally
> but she would be mental.
> How could I live with that?
>
> She died three hours later.
> My mom hugged me and cradled me
> in her arms.
> As if I was the baby that had just died.

My Mom   CHARLETTE HAMAMGIAN, GRADE 1

My mom is kind.
My mom is happy.
My mom is like a
    beautiful rose.
She's so, SO, SO pretty
that I cannot take my eyes
    off her.
Her hair is like red,
    shining berries
that have just been
    washed.
I love my mom.

Untitled   JENNIFER MASCARINAS, GRADE 1

Frightened
Dark
Black
Ghost
Noises
Squeaking
doors
Skeletons
in Halloween
and
Vampires
When am I gonna be
brave?

Friendship Falling Apart   SHERMAINE FANN, GRADE 6

A friendship falling apart
Is a very sad thing you
Feel in your heart.
When you've been friends for so many years,
Shared your joys and your tears,
A friendship falling apart
Is a very sad thing.
It's like a bird who's lost a wing,
A clown who's not smiling,
A window, in so many ways,
Because one time it's fine
And then shattered.

Untitled   LISA LIU, GRADE 1 (TRANSLATED FROM CHINESE)

I like more the community.
With children
I am lonely.

Why Do I Have to Be Alone?   MAGDALA JODESTY, GRADE 4

Why do I have to be alone?
All day.
All night.
I have to think
like a grown-up,
but I am really
a kid.
I watch the kids
play with their
fathers and I wish
I could too.
But someday I will.

Noboby Cares   PETULA MORRISON, GRADE 5

Nobody cares if I fall
Nobody cares if I cry
Nobody cares if I sing
but Everybody cares if I hit them
Nobody cares if I pass
Nobody cares if I fail
Nobody cares if I drown
but Everybody cares if I talk rude to them
Nobody cares if I care
Does anybody care
Yeah! I do

The Cart   CHIP ROPER, GRADE 7

When I was two,
I had a cart,
with two wheels as red as blood.
I hit people with it,
in the shins.
When I did,
I had a big smile on my face,
as big as a half of a moon.

I and Me   CARLO WILLIAMS, GRADE 9

I is a part of me
Likewise me is a part of I.
I love me very much
Likewise me love I very much.
But sometimes I hate me
Because me fail to see
That I is a part of me.
Likewise me hate I
Because me can't tell why
When me is me and I is I.
And sometimes I is jealous of me
Likewise me is jealous of I.
Because I can't be me and me can't be I.

My Heart   DAVE, GRADE 9

My heart feels broken like a crumbled leaf.
To hit my girl was like stealing from a person
in their sleep. When I hit her
my statement was brief.
To find this girl took a very long time.
Now, I'm sorry for what I did.
Now on our relationship
there's a lid.
Me and that girl is now done.
There is no relation.
There is no more fun.

Nylon Love   SABRINA RILEY, GRADE 3

> I have love it stretches
> the reason it stretches is I have a
> lot of love and it goes to
> everyone so I have
> lots and
> lots of
> nylon love

Poem   CHANDRAPAUL, GRADE 7

> beautiful friends
> live farms—tomatoes, potatoes, vegetables,
> cows, chickens, ducks, donkey, horse,
> mango tree, orange tree,
> guava tree,
> cherry tree, sousop tree,
> sheep, goat,
> beech trees,
> we use to
> play ball
> corn, banana
> was a great place
> and a lot of
> my friends
> died from the
> raid.

Apples Insides   JASMINE BRASS, GRADE 1

> Sometimes white like clouds
> Sometimes brown like branches
> Red stars grow there.

My Teacher Is Mad   MAURO ESPINOZA, GRADE 2

My teacher is very mad.
She cracks our heads open,
and to the good banabans
she take their heads and smash them together.
And in all the other classes they
hear Crush Crush Bang Bang
Stop Stop please please stop teacher
stop ouch ouch. Ahhhhhhhh!

School   LILLY ROSENBAUM, GRADE 5

School is like Transylvania
haunted and gross.
It is like someone yelling at you
for ten months.

Teachers are
trained to give
homework, mark report cards and give
detention and give lessons.

Principals are trained
to stay in offices
have meetings
and go to classrooms.

Boys
they are
juvenile delinquents.

Girls
get the upper hand.

Untitled   JUNG, GRADE 6

> Junkie Junkie Junkie how dirty I thought they
> were. I open up my eyes I see them playing with
> mice. I open up my door I see them with
> dirty cloth. Junkie Junkie Junkie I bet they live
> in mud. They're free to go, free to do
> anything they want. I want to act, I want
> to play, I want to be a Junkie.

Things That Have No End   CARLEY ANNE REIDY, GRADE 4

> A circle has no end.
> It just goes round and round.
>
> The lines are endless on a circle.
>
> Space has no end.
> It has a north, a south, an east, and
> a west.
> But soon the north is south
> and east is west and it just
> goes around in a circle.

Dreams Are Gone   MICHAEL LEE, GRADE 9

> Dreams are often washed away.
> Why is that? Shouldn't they be with you
> for awhile?
> Like money, you often have a lot of money
> and then it goes.
> Where has it gone?
> You look around and fine merchandise
> has replaced the money.
> But what has replaced your dreams?

The City Is So Big   RICHARD BYRD, GRADE 8

The city is so big.
Its bridges quake with fear.
I know, I have seen it at night.

The lights sliding from house to house.
And trains pass with windows shiny
like a smile full of teeth.

I have seen machines eating houses.
And stairways walk all by themselves.
And elevator doors opening and closing,
And people disappear.

Sadness of the City   BETHANY JORDAN, GRADE 2

Sadness of the city
O
Sadness of the city
   day and night
      you fall,
   doing things
   to make us cry.
Sadness
   of the city.

Why Do Certain Things Happen When They Do?   SIMONE, GRADE 4

Like why is there good and bad in the world?
Why are countries always fighting?
Why do people give out violence?
Why do things happen when they do?
Like when your parents get upset with you?
Who stirs up people's minds?
When people go hay wire, who does that?

Poem   NOAH BRESLON, GRADE 7

A man and
his trombone
on a street
corner in
New York City.

"An ugly sound,"
they say, but
to me it's music.

The slide moves up and down.
There is nothing like it.
Trumpets have keys.
Clarinets have buttons.
But the trombone is unique.

People ask me
"Noah, how do you know how to move the slide."
I tell them I don't know, my trombone
knows.

The way
a
trombone looks
like no other thing
on earth.

Bibliographies

ANTHOLOGIES AND BOOKS OF POETRY FOR CHILDREN

Adoff, Arnold, ed. *I Am the Darker Brother*. New York: Macmillan, 1968.
A great selection of poems by black American poets.
———. *My Black Me*. New York: E. P. Dutton, 1974.
A beginning book of black poetry by contemporary American poets.
Clifton, Lucille. *Everett Anderson's Year*. New York: Holt, Rinehart & Winston, 1974.
———. *Everett Anderson's Goodbye*. New York: Holt, Rinehart & Winston, 1983.
Two poem-books about a young boy, Everett Anderson, by one of my favorite contemporary poets. These books are especially good for the younger grades.
Dunning, Stephen, Edward Lueders, and Hugh Smith, eds. *Reflections on a Gift of Watermelon Pickle and Other Modern Verse*. Glenview, Ill.: Scott, Foresman, 1966.
An excellent selection of poems on all subjects for upper-grade students especially.
Fleischman, Paul. *Joyful Noise: Poems for Two Voices*. New York: Harper & Row, 1988.
Poems about insects written to be read aloud by two readers.
Frost, Robert. *Birches*. New York: Henry Holt, 1988.

————. *Stopping by Woods on a Snowy Evening*. Illustrated by Susan Jeffers. New York: E. P. Dutton, 1978.

Beautifully illustrated picture-book versions of two of Robert Frost's great poems. I read these books to all grades.

Greenfield, Eloise. *Honey, I Love and Other Love Poems*. New York: Thomas Y. Crowell, 1978.

One of the most popular books in the New York City schools. Eloise Greenfield speaks in her poems about the things she loves in the world.

Hall, Donald. *The Ox-Cart Man*. New York: Puffin Books, 1983.

A picture-book poem set in rural nineteenth-century New England, a favorite with both adults and children.

Hopkins, Lee Bennett, ed. *The Sky Is Full of Song*. New York: Harper & Row, 1983.

Some good poems about the city selected by one of the best anthologists.

————. *A Song in Stone: City Poems*. New York: Thomas Y. Crowell, 1983.

A selection of short poems about the city.

Hughes, Langston. *The Dream Keeper and Other Poems*. New York: Alfred A. Knopf, 1932.

A selection of sixty poems by one of our best American poets.

Janeczko, Paul, ed. *Pocket Poems*. New York: Bradbury, 1985.

Edited by another favorite anthologist, Paul Janeczko, who has chosen good contemporary poems that are small enough to fit in our pockets. Upper-grade and secondary students and teachers love this book.

Jarrell, Randall. *The Bat-Poet*. New York: Macmillan, 1963.

A wonderful story about a bat who finds himself different from his friends—he wakes during the day and writes poetry.

Jordan, June, ed. *Who Look at Me*. New York: Thomas Y. Crowell, 1969.

A long poem by one of my favorite poets. June Jordan says in her introduction to this book, "The question of every desiring heart is, thus, *Who Look at Me?*" The poem is illustrated with a variety of paintings of black American life.

Koch, Kenneth, and Kate Farrell, eds. *Talking to the Sun*. New York: Holt, Rinehart & Winston, 1985.

A beautiful and sophisticated anthology of poems from all times and from all over the world. One of the things that makes this anthology so special is the accompanying works of art from the Metropolitan Museum of Art. For adults and upper grades.

Kuskin, Karla. *Near the Window Tree*. New York: Harper & Row, 1975.
What I love about this book are the notes Karla Kuskin includes with each poem on how she got her ideas. This book is especially good for younger writers and readers.

Livingston, Myra Cohn. *A Circle of Seasons*. New York: Holiday House, 1982.

———. *Celebrations*. New York: Holiday House, 1985.

———. *Earth Songs*. New York: Holiday House, 1986.
All three of these books, from one of the finest children's poets, are filled with poems based on beautiful observations of the things of nature and the universe. The poems are set above and beside rich paintings by Leonard Everett Fisher.

Margolis, Richard. *Secrets of a Small Brother*. New York: Macmillan, 1984.
These short, truthful poems, told from a younger brother's perspective, describe the good and hard times of living with an older brother.

Merriam, Eve. *Rainbow Writing*. New York: Atheneum, 1976.
Poems by the well-known children's poet. I particularly like those about writing, such as "Ways of Composing" and "The Poem as a Door." For upper-grade students.

Moore, Lilian. *I Feel the Same Way*. New York: Atheneum, 1967.
Short, imagistic poems about all kinds of feelings. Especially great for the younger ones.

———. *I Thought I Heard the City Sing*. New York: Atheneum, 1969.
More poems by Lilian Moore about things she's seen in the city, from "Pigeons" to a "Roofscape." Also good for younger students.

Ryder, Joanne. *Inside Turtle's Shell and Other Poems of the Field*. New York: Macmillan, 1985.
Beautiful natural poems. Especially for older children.

Rylant, Cynthia. *Waiting to Waltz*. New York: Bradbury Press, 1984.
Poems about growing up in a small town by one of my favorite children's authors. Upper-grade and secondary students love her poems.

Sandburg, Carl. *Early Moon*. New York: Harcourt Brace Jovanovich, 1958.
A collection of seventy poems by the popular American poet, especially for young readers and writers.

Thurman, Judith. *Flashlight and Other Poems*. New York: Atheneum, 1976.
Short, surprising poems on such unlikely subjects as an "Oilslick" or a "Hydrant." Particularly good for young writers.

Worth, Valerie. *All the Small Poems*. New York: Farrar, Straus & Giroux, 1985.

Small, vivid poems about ordinary things.

Zolotow, Charlotte. *All That Sunlight*. New York: Harper & Row, 1967.

Kindergartners and first graders love these poems, which are short and full of images and music.

REFERENCE BOOKS ON POETRY
AND TEACHING POETRY

Arnstein, Flora. *Poetry and the Child*. (Formerly titled: *Poetry in the Elementary Classroom*.) New York: Dover Publications, 1962.

———. *Children Write Poetry: A Creative Approach*. New York: Dover Publications, 1967.

Flora Arnstein's books were some of my initial inspirations for teaching poetry. They're hard to find, but they give a lot of good ideas on how to teach children poetry.

Koch, Kenneth. *Rose, Where Did You Get that Red? Teaching Great Poetry to Children*. New York: Random House, 1973.

I recommend this book especially for its selection of great poems by poets such as Rimbaud, Dickinson, and D. H. Lawrence.

Livingston, Myra Cohn. *Child as Poet: Myth or Reality*. Boston: Horn Book, 1984.

An excellent and important survey on teaching poetry by one of the virtuosi in the field.

Lopate, Phillip. *Being with Children*. Garden City, New York: Doubleday, 1975.

A fascinating account of teaching poetry in a New York City school.

Mearns, Hughes. *Creative Youth*. Garden City, New York: Doubleday, 1925.

One of the first books I read on teaching, which inspired many good ideas.

Nims, John Frederick. *Western Wind: An Introduction to Poetry*. New York: Random House, 1974.

A great introduction to poetry for advanced upper-grade students and adults.

Padgett, Ron, ed. *Handbook of Poetic Forms*. New York: Teachers & Writers Collaborative, 1987.

A good introduction to poetic forms.

Perrine, Laurence. *Sound and Sense*. New York: Harcourt, Brace & World, 1963.

Another good introductory book on poetry for secondary students and adults.

BOOKS ON THE TEACHING OF WRITING

The following is a selection of recommended readings for teachers who want to learn more about teaching writing in general. Atwell's, Calkins's, and Elbow's books have some information about teaching poetry.

Atwell, Nancie. *In the Middle: Writing, Reading, and Learning with Adolescents*. Portsmouth, N.H.: Boynton/Cook, 1987.

Calkins, Lucy McCormick. *The Art of Teaching Writing*. Portsmouth, N.H.: Heinemann, 1986.

Elbow, Peter. *Writing with Power*. New York: Oxford University Press, 1981.

Graves, Donald. *Writing: Teachers and Children at Work*. Portsmouth, N.H.: Heinemann, 1983.

Murray, Donald. *Learning by Teaching: Selected Articles on Writing and Teaching*. Portsmouth, N.H.: Boynton/Cook, 1982.

———. *Write to Learn*. New York: Holt, Rinehart & Winston, 1984.

Zinsser, William. *On Writing Well: An Informal Guide to Writing Nonfiction*. 3rd ed. New York: Harper & Row, 1985.